Muhammad: A Very Short Introduction

VERY SHORT INTRODUCTIONS are for anyone wanting a stimulating and accessible way in to a new subject. They are written by experts, and have been published in more than 25 languages worldwide.

The series began in 1995, and now represents a wide variety of topics in history, philosophy, religion, science, and the humanities. The VSI Library now contains over 200 volumes—a Very Short Introduction to everything from ancient Egypt and Indian philosophy to conceptual art and cosmology—and will continue to grow to a library of around 300 titles.

Very Short Introductions available now:

For more information visit our web site
www.oup.co.uk/general/vsi/

Jonathan A. C. Brown

MUHAMMAD

A Very Short Introduction

OXFORD
UNIVERSITY PRESS

OXFORD
UNIVERSITY PRESS

Great Clarendon Street, Oxford OX2 6DP

Oxford University Press is a department of the University of Oxford.
It furthers the University's objective of excellence in research, scholarship,
and education by publishing worldwide in

Oxford New York

Auckland Cape Town Dar es Salaam Hong Kong Karachi
Kuala Lumpur Madrid Melbourne Mexico City Nairobi
New Delhi Shanghai Taipei Toronto

With offices in

Argentina Austria Brazil Chile Czech Republic France Greece
Guatemala Hungary Italy Japan Poland Portugal Singapore
South Korea Switzerland Thailand Turkey Ukraine Vietnam

Oxford is a registered trade mark of Oxford University Press
in the UK and in certain other countries

Published in the United States
by Oxford University Press Inc., New York

British Library Cataloguing in Publication Data

Data available

Library of Congress Cataloging in Publication Data

Data available

Typeset by SPI Publisher Services, Pondicherry, India
Printed in Great Britain
on acid-free paper by
Ashford Colour Press Ltd, Gosport, Hampshire

ISBN 978-0-19-955928-2

10

'Let's look it up.'
To my mother Dr Ellen Brown,
who inspired all her children.

Contents

Preface

> Muhammad is not the father of any of your men. Rather he
> is the Messenger of God and the Seal of the Prophets. And
> God is most knowing of all things.
>
> (Quran 33:40)

The task of writing a short biography of Muhammad is relatively
straightforward. As we shall see, there are historiographical
obstacles, but these are par for the course for historians. What
I find truly challenging is to communicate, and to understand
myself, what Muhammad has meant to Muslims over the
centuries.

In the spring of 2006, I participated in a Muslim/Danish dialogue
convened by the Abu Dhabi-based Taba Foundation to address
worldwide Muslim anger over a Danish newspaper's publication
of caricatures of Muhammad. A number of the Danish delegates
told me that they did not understand how *any* historical figure,
even a religious icon like Muhammad, could mean so much to
people that they would take to the streets in protest of pictures
defaming him or her.

Trying to explain such extraordinary affection, I replied that, for
the past fourteen centuries, Muhammad has been the intimate
companion of the believers. In the Prophet's Mosque in Medina,

he lies buried in the earth behind an ornately wrought grill. Muslim pilgrims grasp furtively at the metal bars, hoping to inch closer to their Prophet. Their words ring out: 'May God's peace and blessings be upon you, O Messenger of God!', an Egyptian man cries out to the grave. An elderly Indian man in a wheelchair struggles vainly with the guards and family members; he calls out to God to take his life here and let him be buried in Medina, 'the City of the Messenger of God'. One man mutters emotively, 'I am here, O Messenger of God. Are you proud of me? I am one of your followers . . .'.

I do not think, however, that my explanation sufficed. As powerful as such scenes are, there is something even greater and more communally binding about the person of Muhammad. For the past few days, I have been asking Indonesian Muslims of all ages and walks of life what Muhammad means to them. They have all responded with the same telltale sense of ownership and identification: 'He is *our* dear Prophet.'

It is perhaps in this sense of being 'our' Prophet, part of 'us' and how we understand 'our' identity as Muslims, that the secret of Muhammad's tremendous import lies. His image is inscribed in the hearts of the believers by the spirit of faith and bonds of community. He is a light kindled in a Muslim's heart from a young age through family and education, regardless of the tremendous diversity of Muslim cultures and lifestyles. Like all light, the Prophet's indispensability is only realized when it is gone, and Muslims' need for it only heard when someone reaches to take it away.

Jonathan A. C. Brown
Yogyakarta, Indonesia
29 June 2009

Acknowledgements

First, I must thank Oxford University Press and the editors of its remarkable *Very Short Introductions* series for giving me the opportunity to contribute this volume. I am grateful to a perennially giving mentor, John Esposito, for encouraging me to take up this project.

In my overall approach to writing about Muhammad, I am deeply indebted to three teachers. Dr Tareq al-Suwaidan taught me the importance of good storytelling – I hope that my rendition of this story suits the immensity of its content. Ali Zayn al-Abidin al-Jifri guided me on the path towards understanding what Muhammad has meant to Muslims throughout the centuries – I hope to succeed in communicating this to a general audience in such a slim volume. Dr Fred Donner introduced me to the great historiographical debates surrounding the historical Muhammad and fostered in me a burning interest in historiography – I hope that readers glean from this book a sense of the challenges we face when we speak of the past.

I am also very grateful to my many colleagues and friends who assisted me in my research and writing: Dr Scott Lucas (as usual), Dr Todd Linafelt, Dr Ahmed El Shamsy, Dr Joel Walker, Rodrigo Adem, my students at the University of Washington, and the UW's venerable Historians' Reading Group. Sohaira

Siddiqui deserves special credit for helping me scan the vast literature on Muhammad. I must thank Saima Haqq, Hussein Rashid, and Asad Naqvi for helping with the section on Qawwali.

I dedicated this book to my mother, Dr Ellen Brown, because she was my first and greatest teacher. She died suddenly in June 2010 in Addis Ababa (having seen the dedication), and as the book goes to press, I take this opportunity to offer what encomium I can. My mother was above all a great scholar. She was an anthropologist committed to understanding the true nature of human society, a compelling writer, a woman of piercing intellect and encyclopaedic knowledge, a clever critic, and the toughest and most resourceful person I have encountered. She spent a career travelling alone through the boiling African Sahel and overcame excruciating illnesses, all the while treating those around her with compassion. She was an effulgently and endlessly loving mother, a loyal friend, a consummate chef, and a moral exemplar to all who knew her. She was a generous soul who sought always to do good and to improve the lives of others. If I have accomplished anything in this book, the bulk of the credit is hers. I do not think that her children or those who knew her well can ever fully express how much they love her and how proud they are of her. She will remain the best and wisest person I have ever known.

I also extend my sincere thanks to all my family and friends. I am particularly grateful to my father, Jonathan C. Brown, for always supporting my endeavours and encouraging me to write books that the public might actually read. I feel a strong need, at this point in my life, to thank a group of Washington DC families who have provided an extension of my own family: the Tafts, Samuels, Stevensons, Holts, and Woolseys. I have longed aspired to the standards of excellence that this extended family has provided with such seeming ease throughout my life. To my wife Laila, I owe a special debt. Throughout my months of writing this book, I hoped more than anything that she would be proud of the result.

Note on transliteration and names

Most of the foreign words in this book originally come from Arabic. I have tried to use a system of transliteration that will assist readers with pronunciation without exceeding the mandate of an introductory text. In the foreign words in this book, the letter 'q' indicates an 'emphatic uvular stop' similar to the 'c' sound in the crowing sound 'caw caw'. 'Dh' indicates the 'th' sound in words like 'bother'. The symbol ' indicates the Arabic letter *ayn*, which does not exist in English but sounds like the 'aaah' sound one makes when having one's throat checked by a doctor. 'Kh' indicates the sound one would make when clearing one's throat or a 'j' in the Spanish name 'Jose', and 'gh' resembles the French 'r' in words like 'Paris'.

In Arabic names, 'Ibn' or 'bin' mean 'son of'. 'Abu' means 'father of', and 'Umm' means 'mother of'. In Arabic names, it is common to refer to someone as 'father of so-and-so' or 'mother of so-and-so' as a nickname. 'Banu' means 'sons of', and is used to refer to a tribe.

List of illustrations

Chapter 1
The life of the Messenger of God

Caveat: legend and fact

There are tremendous challenges to telling religious stories in which myth and fact mix so freely and so clearly depend on one's point of view. If we believe the sacred history told by the followers of a religious figure like Muhammad, then we are uncritically accepting their religion as true. But if we ignore the pious legend that surrounds such a person and are only interested in 'what really happened', then we neglect the tremendous importance that such legends have held for the followers of that faith throughout history.

Since legend is just as important as fact in appreciating Muhammad's global importance, and since facts cannot be discovered unless we begin with legend, we will start this book with the Muslim sacred narrative of Muhammad's life. In Chapter 2, we will engage this sacred narrative to see whence it emerged and how it was formed.

Of course, there is no one, official version of Muhammad's life even amongst Muslims, who agree on its broad narrative but differ on many of its details. The schism between Shiite and Sunni Muslims, for example, has its roots in different accounts of Muhammad's words and teachings. Here we will try to present an ecumenical version of Muhammad's life that balances between these different

Muslim accounts and also stays true to the earliest authoritative Muslim biographies of Muhammad, 'the Prophet' and 'Messenger of God'. Do not be surprised by the reverent tone of the section that follows – you are stepping into Muslim shoes now.

Life on the edge of the desert and the verge of prophecy

Arriving on the Red Sea coast of Arabia in the year 570 CE, you would find it a desolate land. The sweltering heat and humidity of the coast lose none of their strength as you climb the slow and steady slope to the low, craggy mountains of the Hejaz (see Figure 1). Even the steep and black rocky hills seem to wither

1. **The Arabian Peninsula and environs c. 600 CE**

under the powerful sun, interspacing yellow tracts of sand and occasional shrubs. Further east, over the horizon and beyond the mountains, lie the deserts and oases of the plain of Najd.

Arabia from the Red Sea across Najd to the Persian Gulf is a land where water is so scarce that life hardly seems possible. There are no rivers, no lakes. Crops, beasts, and men drink only from the wells and scattered oases, which draw life from the occasional torrential rains, sudden downpours which turn valleys into gushing rivers driving all before them. Date palms, with their small, sweet fruit, and livestock sustain life. The people settled around the oases and wells rely on the Arab Bedouins of the deserts for meat and animal hides, and the Bedouins cannot survive without the meagre crops and crafts of the settled Arabs. The camel, the 'ship of the desert', the sheep, and the herd dog are the inseparable companions of men.

So are the sword and the bow. The people who live in the craggy valleys of the Hejaz and the plains of Najd live always on the verge of famine, drought, and death. It is a harsh life in which only kinship affords protection from raiding by other tribes and only honour in battle gives immortality. There is no government, no law, only family and the tribe. There are no written histories, only the recited poems of deeds done in battle and lost desert loves.

To the north, beyond the deserts, lie the great empires of the civilized world. The Byzantine Roman Empire, Greek in culture and Christian in religion, rules the rich cities of the Levantine coast and Egypt. The Persian Sassanian Empire, whose 'King of Kings' sat enthroned beneath a gold crown so heavy it had to be suspended by a thin cord from the ceiling, ruled the fertile flood plain of Iraq and the hilly plateau of Iran. The Persians, who mainly followed the religion of the ancient prophet Zoroaster, ruled over populations of Christians, Jews, and even Buddhists.

To the south, the highlands of Yemen are a different world. Yemen's cool mountains and terraced, cultivated hillsides seem like a paradise compared to central Arabia. Daily rains feed grain and precious myrrh crops alike, and Yemeni spices are prized from the Mediterranean world to India. The Sassanian Empire and the Ethiopian Christian allies of Byzantium vie for control over this valuable country, and it trades hands between them. In the shadow of these great powers during the previous two centuries, the old gods of the cities and tribes of Yemen had given way to monotheism: Judaism and Christianity.

Yet you would think that the God of Abraham and Jesus had no care for Arabia. Except for some powerful Jewish tribes and scattered converts to Christianity and Zoroastrianism, the Arabs of the Hejaz were polytheists, praying to the idols of their tribes and families to protect them from the harsh elements. But the Arabs also nurtured an ancient legend of the one God, the God of Abraham: He had buried a spiritual treasure in the mountains of the Hejaz, in a small town located at the intersection of four narrow, rocky valleys. Here in Mecca lay the foundations of the Kaba, the shrine built ages ago by Abraham as 'the first house of worship appointed for men' (Quran 3:96).

As legend held, Abraham and his wife Sarah had been childless. Yet Sarah's bondswoman Hagar bore Abraham a son, Ismail (Ishmael). When Sarah herself gave birth to Isaac soon after, God instructed Abraham to take Hagar and Ismail south to Mecca, where the mother and child could settle. Left on their own, Hagar ran back and forth between two hills in Mecca frantically searching for water. Her young son Ismail, guided by God, dug his heel into the earth and up bubbled the cool spring of Zamzam. Ismail and Hagar joined a tribe of Arabs who dwelt near Mecca, and from time to time Abraham would visit them. One year, God instructed Abraham and Ismail to build a house of worship for Him in Mecca: a square building of

4

stone, inserting in one of its corners a jet-black stone that had fallen from heaven itself.

The valley of Mecca would be a sacred sanctuary, where neither hunting nor fighting would be allowed. With the Kaba built, God ordered Abraham 'to proclaim the Pilgrimage (*hajj*) among men – they will come to thee on foot and mounted on every kind of beast, lean from journeying, from deep and distant mountain highways' (Quran 22:27). The Kaba would be the centre of worship of the one true God. More, it was the centre of the world and the very contact point between earth and heaven.

Over the years, however, the Arabs corrupted the pure monotheism of Abraham. Perhaps there was one great God who created and sustained the world, but surely lesser gods existed in certain places and for certain peoples to govern their affairs. These gods dwelt in statues and stones and in specific shrines. The descendants of Ismail left Mecca, taking rocks from the sacred precinct around the Kaba and making them their tribal idols. Other Arabs began worshipping images of their ancestors as gods. Soon each tribe had its own gods, and in towns such as Yathrib in the Hejaz each household had its own guardian spirits.

Legend told that new tribes came to Mecca and set up their idols around the Kaba. One Meccan travelled to Syria and brought back a great golden idol, Hubal, which was placed inside the Kaba. The Zamzam well silted over and was buried. The Kaba itself fell into disrepair, and the Jews, descended from Abraham's son Isaac, stopped attending the yearly pilgrimage to Mecca. But still the Arabs would come yearly to honour the Kaba and the one great God, Allah ('The God'), whom they acknowledged to be in command even over their tribal and local gods. Moreover, merchants flocked to the annual pilgrimage, and goods and monies traded hands as quickly as prayers issued forth from lips.

The idols and gods worshipped by the Arabs provided them with no ethics or morals. They merely wanted sacrifices and ritual invocations. The morals of the Arabs came from their notion of honour and virtue, *muruwwa*. Values such as courage in battle, generosity to guests, and duty to the tribe meant all. Arab morality was one of hyperbole, stretched between two poles of *jahl*, the proud and unrestrained honour of a warrior, and *hilm*, the sound reason and calm deliberation of a chief. The Arabs' poetry celebrated both virtues. One poet wrote of *jahl*:

> Let no one deal brashly with us, for we'll respond with a brashness
> Which dwarfs even the brashest of the brash.

Another wrote of *hilm*:

> He who does not deal craftily in matters will be ground down
> By the camel's molars and crushed by its hooves.

The Arabs were resigned to their fate of raiding and fighting amongst tribes for spoils and glory. As one poet sang:

> No denying that we are meat for the sword, nor do we deny that we
> Feed it meat as well from time to time.

Eventually, a new tribe gained supremacy in Mecca: the Quraysh (The Association). Of the clans within the Quraysh, three were particularly wealthy and powerful: the Banu Hashim (Sons of Hashim), the Banu Umayya (Sons of Umayya), and the Banu Makhzum (Sons of Makhzum). There were other branches of the tribe as well, like Taym and 'Adi, which were less prominent. Arabs from other tribes who came and settled in Mecca could become clients of Quraysh clans, and the wealthy Quraysh held many Ethiopian slaves.

The Quraysh were businessmen above all else, settled Arabs who made their living through caravans sent north to Syria and south to

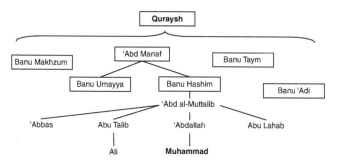

2. Major clans of the Quraysh and their relations

Yemen as well as through trade with the Bedouin Arabs. The Meccan sanctuary of the Kaba was also a major source of income. The Quraysh maintained 360 idols standing around the Kaba, placed there by the tribes of Arabia. The most renowned of these was the goddess 'Uzza of the Khuza'a tribe. The mighty golden god Hubal resided safely inside the Kaba, where the Meccans also placed a painting of Jesus and Mary to accommodate the occasional Christian who passed through Mecca. There were other sanctuaries in Arabia, to be sure: the sanctuary of the goddess Lat in the nearby city of Ta'if to the south, and the goddess Manat near the Red Sea coast.

Not all the Arabs had forgotten the monotheism of Abraham, however. A few individuals, known as *hanif*s, turned away from the practices of their tribes to meditate in the desert and worship the one true God. They were often shunned by their polytheist kin, and one famous *hanif* of Mecca found himself exiled from his home town and forced to wander Arabia until his death.

But even among the mercantile Quraysh, life was austere. Their caravans carried not precious spices, but rough goods like animal hides and butter. The finest food in Mecca was a meat soup with bread slices in it.

In the mid-500s, great upheavals seemed to hang in the air. 'Abd al-Muttalib, the chief of the Banu Hashim clan and a powerful leader in the Quraysh, had a dream in which he was guided to dig near the Kaba. There he rediscovered the ancient Zamzam well. Soon the Kaba itself would be rebuilt anew, its roof timbers taken from a shipwreck on the Red Sea coast.

When Christian converts in the city of Najran, on the border between the mountains of Yemen and the Hejaz, were martyred by the Jewish king of the city, a Christian army from Ethiopia occupied Yemen. The Ethiopians transformed a shrine in the Yemeni city of Sanaa into a church, which quickly became a pilgrimage centre. An Arab related to the Quraysh saw this as a threat to the primacy of the Meccan sanctuary and travelled to Sanaa to pay homage to this church – by defecating in it. Incensed, the Ethiopian governor of Yemen launched a campaign against Mecca. Little did he know that he was attacking the land that would soon give birth to God's final prophet.

Portents and the birth of a prophet

The Quraysh called that year, 570 CE, the Year of the Elephant, because the great Ethiopian host that converged on Mecca contained a number of war elephants. Upon reaching the outskirts of the town, however, the elephants of the Ethiopian army mysteriously would go no further. More miraculous was the aid that the Quraysh received next. A vast flock of birds swooped down upon the Ethiopians, pelting them with stones held in their claws and beaks. The Ethiopian army was wracked by a horrendous plague and quickly retreated.

The miraculous victory was but one portent, however, of the seminal event to come that year. Some months earlier, 'Abd al-Muttalib had taken his son 'Abdallah to find a wife amongst the tribes living in the town of Yathrib to the north of Mecca.

One woman named Qutayla, well versed in soothsaying, saw 'Abdallah pass by and sensed a luminousness about the young man. She hoped he might take her as his mate. But 'Abdallah was to be married to a woman named Amina. After the wedding night, as he took Amina back to Mecca, 'Abdallah was again approached by Qutayla. This time, however, she sensed that the luminescence had passed from him.

Amina soon found herself with child. But she learned quickly that her son would be no ordinary man. One night she heard voices saying, 'You carry in your womb the lord of his people, and when he is born say, "I place him in the protection of the one God, from the evil of the enviers", then name him "the Most Praised (Muhammad)".' Sometimes it was as if she saw lights emanating from her belly and illuminating the distant castles of Syria. The night Amina gave birth to her son, the stars seemed to descend to the earth from the sky. Even at his birth, her son, Muhammad, spread his hands on the earth and raised his head to the heavens.

Others knew of Muhammad's birth as well. Some of the rabbis of the Jewish tribes in Yathrib knew from their scriptures that a prophet was to come among the Arabs. On the night of Muhammad's birth, in Yathrib one rabbi stood atop a hill and called out, 'Under this star shall be born The Most Praised (Ahmad, an alternative name for Muhammad).' But the rabbi's people did not heed him.

Muhammad's father 'Abdallah died before he was born, and being fatherless was a great shame amongst the Arabs. In Mecca, young children were usually given to milk-mothers from the Bedouin Arabs. These infants would spend the first few years of life in the clean desert air tending herds. A woman named Halima agreed to take Muhammad and wean him, sending him back to Mecca occasionally to visit his mother Amina.

One day, the children who were tending the herds with Muhammad ran back to Halima with a terrifying story: Muhammad had been attacked and killed by two strangers clad in white! When Muhammad returned alive and well, he explained that these two figures had split open his chest and removed his heart, washing it in a silver basin filled with pure snow and removing from it a black dot. Then they had replaced his heart and placed between his shoulders a seal, a small round bump. When Amina heard this news, she knew that the portents of Muhammad's birth were being fulfilled.

Amina died when her son was only six years old, and Muhammad then came under the care of his grandfather, the wise 'Abd al-Muttalib. For two years, Muhammad sat with his grandfather, the chief of the Banu Hashim clan, seeing how a leader conducted himself and arbitrated the disputes of others. When 'Abd al-Muttalib died, Muhammad's paternal uncle Abu Talib assumed leadership of the clan and took Muhammad into his care. Muhammad accompanied his uncle on his caravan journeys north into Syria.

During one trip to the north a remarkable incident occurred. The caravan passed by a monk's desert retreat as it made its way along the highway. When the Arabs stopped to rest, the monk, a Christian named Bahira, noticed that a cloud shaded them as they walked. When the adults of the group came to greet the monk, Bahira noticed that the cloud hovered over a boy who remained with the caravan. He called to the boy and examined him. Finding the seal of prophecy between his shoulders, he knew that this was the prophet whom his Christian scriptures had foretold: he was the Paraclete, the 'Comforter and Most Praised' that the true teachings of Jesus had predicted would come. Bahira informed Abu Talib of Muhammad's destiny, warning him to beware the Jews of Arabia, who would seek to harm a non-Jewish prophet.

As Muhammad grew to adulthood, he came to be admired and respected by all the Quraysh. He was known as *al-Amin*, 'the Trustworthy', and people left their money and goods in his care when they travelled. He participated in the wars the Quraysh fought even as a teenager, picking up arrows from the battlefield so that the Quraysh could shoot them back at the enemy. When the Quraysh decided to rebuild the Kaba, it was Muhammad's insight that overcame internecine tensions. With the Kaba almost complete, the clans of Quraysh vied with one another over who should lift the final stone into place. Muhammad suggested that all the clans lift the stone together on a cloak.

As an orphan, with no father to honour him, Muhammad married late compared to most of his friends. When he was 25, Muhammad was approached by Khadija, a wealthy widow 15 years his senior. She offered him marriage and a business partnership. Muhammad took over management of Khadija's caravans, and the two became loving partners.

Muhammad would have no other wives until Khadija died. She bore Muhammad four daughters, Ruqayya, Zaynab, Umm Kulthum, and Fatima, as well as one son named al-Qasim. Sadly, al-Qasim died while still a baby. Muhammad was destined to have no sons survive infancy. 'Zaynab gave birth to a daughter who survived, Umama'. Fatima would eventually wed Muhammad's young cousin Ali, and the couple would produce Muhammad's only grandsons, al-Hasan and al-Husayn, along with two granddaughters, named for their aunts Zaynab and Umm Kulthum.

As the years passed and his caravans yielded a livelihood, Muhammad took to meditating in the desert and rocky mountain caves outside of Mecca. He had never participated in the worship of his tribe's gods or sacrificed meat to their idols. Nor had he ever taken part in the rowdy dancing at weddings. As a youth, he had once gone to watch a ceremony but had strangely been lulled to sleep outside.

Something had always drawn him away from and above these false gods towards the power he felt so keenly in the desert, between the earth and the majestic night sky. In time, he began having wondrous dreams in which angels and omens appeared to him, and his meditations seemed to bring him closer to some great consequence.

The beginning of revelation

In 610 CE, when Muhammad was 40 years old, his first revelation came. Sitting alone in the cave of Hira in a mountain above Mecca, a figure appeared to him in a blaze of glory. 'Read!' the figure commanded him. 'How am I to read?' Muhammad replied – he was illiterate. The figure embraced Muhammad tightly and again said, 'Read!'. 'How am I to read?' he again replied, terrified. The figure embraced him again, this time so forcefully that Muhammad thought he would be crushed. The heavenly figure then recited:

> Read in the name of your Lord who created,
> Created man from an embedded clot.
> Read, for your Lord is the most bounteous,
> Who taught by the pen,
> Taught man what he did not know.
>
> (Quran 96:1–5)

So began the Quran, 'The Recitation', and the prophethood of God's final messenger to mankind. That destiny had yet to unfold, however, and at that moment Muhammad was overcome with terror. What had just happened? Was he mad? He hurried down the rocky slope towards the lit houses of Mecca. What would his tribe say if he told them of this? Surely he was insane or possessed. He considered throwing himself off the mountain, but suddenly the figure appeared again to him in the form of a man who stood astride the horizon. 'O Muhammad, you are the messenger of God, and I am the archangel Gabriel', it proclaimed.

Muhammad struggled back to Khadija and told her 'Indeed, I hear a voice and see a light, and I fear that I am mad.' She comforted him, saying 'God would never afflict you with this, since you are known for your truthfulness, character and kindness.' Khadija took Muhammad to see her cousin, Waraqa, a Christian who was well versed in the scriptures.

Upon hearing what had happened, Waraqa rejoiced – he knew that this event was foretold in the scriptures and comforted Muhammad by telling him that the angel that had appeared to Moses in ancient days had now come to him. He would be the prophet of his people. More, he would be the prophet sent to all mankind, 'a mercy to all the worlds' (Quran 21:107).

As the months passed, the angel appeared to Muhammad again with more revelations, comforting him. One revelation read:

> By the bright morning hours, and the night as it fades away, your Lord has not forsaken you, nor does He despise you. Surely the future is better for you than the past, and then will your Lord grant you, and you shall be well pleased. Did He not find you an orphan and shelter you? Find you lost and guide you? Find you poor and enrich you?

(Quran 93:1–8)

Another read:

> By the pen and what is written, you are not, by the bounty of your Lord, mad.

(Quran 68:1–3)

Far from insanity, Muhammad knew from Gabriel that the words he was hearing were the words of the one God Himself, 'the creator and sustainer of all the worlds'. The Quran was the word of God, communicated by Gabriel to the Prophet and spoken to the people in his human voice. When God revealed verses of the Quran to Muhammad, sometimes his followers could hear a sound like the buzzing of bees around his face. Sometimes, the stress of the revelation would make him break into a sweat even on the coldest days, and he would be seized with a headache. Sometimes, the experience was so overpowering that it left Muhammad dazed, and more than once he passed out from the strain.

God could reveal verses of the Quran, or even whole chapters, without any obvious incitement. But often the revelation would come to answer some pressing question presented to the Prophet by a follower or a new challenge facing his community. Although Muhammad himself was illiterate, he would dictate the Quran to his scribes, who would set it down on primitive writing materials.

Khadija had believed Muhammad the moment he had told her of his experience, and his close friend Abu Bakr and young cousin Ali, the ten-year-old son of the Quraysh chief Abu Talib, both believed him as well. They knew Muhammad would never lie, and they pledged themselves to follow whatever he taught. The core of the Muslim community had been formed.

The camps form: conversion and opponents

Muhammad was cautious in his initial preaching, and for three years he did not preach openly. The message that God had revealed to him was simple: 'submission' (*Islam*) to the one God. Islam taught people to turn away from idolatry to the sole worship of the one true God, the Creator, the Shaper, the First and Last, the Knower of All Things; to forget superstitions and customs considered sacred and heed God's revelation; to do good deeds and prepare for the Day of Judgement to come.

In time, God ordered Muhammad to 'rise and warn' and to 'warn your near of kin' (Quran 74:2; 26:214), so he invited the Banu

14

Hashim to a meal at his home. Although there was only a small amount of food there, it miraculously sufficed for all. When Muhammad explained the new religion and asked which of his kin would support his mission to the other clans and be 'my brother, trustee and representative after me among you', no one but the faithful Ali took up the challenge.

A core group of converts to Islam formed around Muhammad, now called 'the Prophet' and 'Messenger of God' by his followers, in the early years of the revelation. They formed the nucleus of what later Muslims would call 'the Companions', or the first generation of Muslims who lived with and knew Muhammad.

Early Companions included Zayd bin al-Haritha, who had been a slave captured by the Quraysh whom Muhammad had adopted as his son. He quickly converted to Islam, and when his own father came to Mecca to reclaim him, Zayd said he would prefer to stay with God's Messenger. A wealthy young man from the Banu Umayya, Uthman, embraced Islam after a dream guided him to Muhammad's teachings. Al-Zubayr, Muhammad's cousin and Abu Bakr's son-in-law, soon converted, as did Abu Bakr's friend and kinsman 'Abd al-Rahman bin 'Awf. Talha, another kinsman of Abu Bakr, converted to Islam after meeting a monk in Syria who described the Arabian prophet foretold in the Christian scriptures. A young Bedouin who had become a client of the Quraysh, 'Abdallah bin Masud, accepted Muhammad's message when the Prophet made a young ewe's udder miraculously swell with milk so that they could drink.

Besides Muhammad's charisma and reputation, perhaps the strongest draw to Islam was the beauty of the Quran itself. The Arabic recitations revealed to Muhammad were so melodious and rich that the Arab ear, so well attuned to poetry, found it irresistible. One man, the chief of the distant tribe of Daws, became Muslim when visiting Mecca after hearing Muhammad recite the Quran.

The new religion of Islam, however, was rejected by most of the Quraysh. The most powerful figures in the tribe formed a solid wall of opposition to Muhammad and his message. Al-Walid bin Mughira, his son Khalid, and the powerful Abu Jahl were leading men of the influential Banu Makhzum clan who aligned themselves squarely against this upstart religion. A man named 'Utba bin Rabi'a also took up the cause against Muhammad, as did his son-in-law, a rising leader in the Banu Umayya named Abu Sufyan. Muhammad's own paternal uncle, Abu Lahab of the Banu Hashim, also became one of his fiercest opponents.

Muhammad's new religion threatened the livelihood of the Quraysh. They derived much of their income from the annual pilgrimage to Mecca, when tribes from all over Arabia came to honour the idols at the Kaba.

Islam also insulted the traditions of the Arabs. Muhammad's demand that they cease worshipping their tribal gods and turn only to the great God broke with generations of tradition. In God's revelations in the Quran, He stated that those tribal gods 'are but names that you and your forefathers have invented' (Quran 53:23), and that people who follow such baseless ideas about the supernatural 'have no knowledge of these things, they do but speculate' (Quran 45:24). In a world with no laws and no government, where security came only from the tribe and its values, turning against the ways of one's ancestors was tantamount to treason. As the Quraysh leaders objected, 'By God we cannot abide our ancestors being insulted, our customs being mocked and our gods being reviled.'

But Muhammad had an influential protector. Although he never became Muslim himself, Abu Talib, the Prophet's uncle and chief of the Banu Hashim, offered Muhammad the protection of his clan against these opponents.

As the number of Muhammad's followers grew, the Quraysh tried to negotiate with him to cease his preaching. But neither offers of money nor power persuaded the Prophet. Muhammad told his opponents that he would not abandon the mission given him by God, 'even if you put the sun in my right hand and the moon in my left'.

Most of Muhammad's followers came from the poorer branches of the Quraysh or from amongst the tribe's slaves, but a number of young, prominent men like Uthman converted as well. In Islam, however, race or wealth did not matter. As the Quran stated, 'The most noble amongst you in the eyes of God is the most pious' (Quran 49:13).

The new religion of Islam seemed to be threatening family ties, the one real institution of Arabian society. Abu Bakr's own son, 'Abd al-Kaba, refused to become Muslim, while the daughter of Abu Sufyan, a leading opponent of Muhammad, embraced Islam. In the bosom of the Banu Makhzum clan, whose leaders despised Muhammad's message, two members of the clan, Yasir and his wife, converted despite family resistance. Later, when an angry Quraysh man said he wanted to kill Muhammad, it was because 'he is the one who has split the Quraysh in two'. Ironically, this man was Umar bin al-Khattab, who would one day lead the Muslim community.

The Quraysh leaders levelled many accusations against Muhammad. They called him a *kahin*, or one of the Arab soothsayers who predicted the future in rhymed prose similar to the prose of the Quran. They accused Muhammad of taking his teachings from a foreigner, a Persian or a Byzantine slave who fed him religious ideas from Christianity or Zoroastrianism. Sometimes they accused Muhammad of being possessed by a *jinn* (a desert spirit, and root of the English word 'genie'). Others accused him of being a poet concocting the verses of the Quran, since in Arabia poets were the propagandists of a tribe who would weave verses to mock enemies or praise heroes.

The Quraysh were in a quandary. Everyone knew Muhammad was supremely trustworthy, and no one could imagine him lying – a fact which Muhammad hoped would convince his stubborn adversaries. One day, he climbed up on a steep hill outside the Kaba and called to the assembled elders of Quraysh, 'If I told you an army were coming over that hill, would you believe me?' When they said yes, he asked them why they would not believe that he brought a message from God. Abu Jahl knew that accusing Muhammad of deception would convince no one, so he said, 'We are not calling you a liar, but rather we are disbelieving in what you've brought.'

When it became clear to the Quraysh that during the annual pilgrimage and market Muhammad and his followers might preach to the visiting Arabs, they decided to tell all the arriving pilgrims that Muhammed was a sorcerer whose magic split people away from their families.

As several years passed and it became clear that Islam was becoming more and more appealing in Mecca, the Quraysh opponents of Muhammad began persecuting Muslims violently. Members of prominent clans like the Banu Hashim were safe from physical harm as long as their clan protected them. It was the poor and disenfranchised who suffered the worst. Abu Jahl, a leader of the Banu Makhzum clan, decided that his kin would not live as Muslims. He tortured his kinsman Yasir and his wife Sumayya, trying to force them to recant. Eventually, Sumayya died under torture. She was the first martyr in Islam. The powerful and gruff young leader of the 'Adi clan, Umar bin al-Khattab, beat Abu Bakr's Muslim slave girl, and another Quraysh leader tortured an Ethiopian slave, a man named Bilal, hoping that he would acknowledge the goddesses Lat and 'Uzza. As Bilal's torturers piled heavy rocks on his chest in the blazing desert sun, he repeated only 'God is one, one, one God.'

Abu Jahl eventually organized a boycott of Muhammad's clan, the Banu Hashim, because its leader Abu Talib would not force him to cease preaching. According to these sanctions, none of the other Quraysh clans could trade or marry with the Banu Hashim. But after two difficult years, the boycott dissolved. The family relations between clans and the solidarity of the Quraysh made isolating one clan impossible.

The Muslims did not want to fight those who despised them or rejected Islam, for the Quran had ordered Muhammad to 'call to the path of your Lord with wisdom and goodly preaching, and dispute with them in the best way' (Quran 16:125). The Muslims were instructed by God to tell their enemies that 'there is no compulsion in religion' (Quran 2:256), 'to you your religion, and to me mine' (Quran 109:6).

Muhammad was often personally taunted and mocked. Once a woman threw a sheep's uterus at him while he was praying, and one day a woman dumped garbage on him. But he was physically safe thanks to the powerful protection of his uncle Abu Talib. The Prophet's real torture was psychological. Every day he saw men and women mocked or beaten because of *his* message, because they believed *he* was God's messenger.

Eventually, the persecution became so severe that Muhammad decided to send those followers of his who were able across the Red Sea to Ethiopia, where a righteous Christian king known as the Negus would shelter them. Al-Zubayr, Uthman, and 81 other Muslim men went along with their wives and children.

When the Muslims arrived, they explained their religion to the king (old Ethiopic was a language very similar to Arabic). They recounted how before they had followed the barbaric customs of

their people, allowing the rich to exploit the poor and committing
the abomination of idolatry. When the Christian Negus asked
them what Muslims believed about Jesus, they read him verses of
the Quran that explained that Jesus was 'a word from the Lord',
a noble prophet, and a servant of God. The Negus was moved to
tears, acknowledging to himself that Jesus and Muhammad
had been sent by the same God. Although the Negus knew that
Jesus was not the son of God, but merely a prophet like
Muhammad, he could not make this public or his Christian
population would revolt. Years later, when the Negus died,
Muhammad would pray for him as a Muslim.

Meanwhile, in Mecca the Muslims continued to worship
privately in the house of a wealthy convert. Only during the four
months that the Arabs considered sacred and during which
warfare was prohibited could they move about the city unmolested.
One day, as the Prophet stood by the Kaba praying, some of the
Meccan elite began to abuse him harshly. They stopped when they
saw a man approaching, a member of the Banu Hashim whom
all respected and feared, Muhammad's powerful uncle Hamza.
'Do you mock the religion of Muhammad', Hamza asked them
gruffly, 'when it is what *I* follow?' No one could respond.

The only man of the Quraysh who was Hamza's equal in strength
and force of personality was Umar bin al-Khattab. Hearing one
day that his own sister had become Muslim, Umar rushed to her
house where he found her and her husband reading a page of the
Quran. He seized it and read the first verse: 'O man! We did not
bestow this Quran upon you to burden you, but as an
exhortation for those who fear God' (Quran 20:1–3). Umar's soul
tumbled inside him at the beauty of the language. God's light
illuminated him, and he announced that he too was a Muslim.

With two powerful supporters in Hamza and Umar, the Prophet
and the Muslims felt confidence for the first time. They left their
refuge and walked in two lines, one lead by Umar and the other

by Hamza, with Muhammad in the middle, towards the Kaba to pray there as a group in the open for the first time.

The Year of Sadness and the night journey to Jerusalem

Muhammad claimed to be a prophet like Noah, Moses, and Jesus, sent with the same message and to call Jews, Christians, and pagans to the one God of Abraham. The Quran referred to the Christians, Jews, and Zoroastrians, whose religions were based on the teachings of true prophets like Moses and Jesus but who had corrupted their beliefs, as 'People of the Book'.

If Muhammad were really a messenger of God like earlier prophets, he would have access to sacred, revealed secrets known to the People of the Book alone. Muhammad's Meccan opponents thought that they could enlist Jews from the city of Yathrib to the north to test Muhammad and expose him as an imposter.

The rabbis sent three questions for Muhammad to answer: what is the nature of the soul?; who was 'He of the Two Horns'?; and how many were the legendary 'People of the Cave'? God revealed verses of the Quran to answer these questions. 'As for the soul', God revealed, '[say, O Muhammad]: "It is a matter of my Lord", and We have not given you knowledge of it except a little' (Quran 17:85). As for the mythical figure known as 'He of the Two Horns', Muhammad explained that he was an ancient conqueror who had mastered the world east and west (he is often associated with Alexander the Great). As for the Companions of the Cave, the Quran explained that these were young men who believed in God but lived in a time of iniquity (it is believed that they were 3rd-century Christians living under Roman persecution). They sought refuge in a cave, where God allowed them to sleep miraculously for decades until they were free to worship God safely. The Quran explained that their number, which some

21

claimed was three, others four, five, or seven, did not matter. It was all idle guessing. Only God knows such things, and men should not speculate about trivialities.

Muhammad had answered the questions correctly. Not only did he know details of the debates around the issues (for example, the different claims about the numbers of those in the cave, and whether or not their dog was counted), he knew the true answer: speculating about questions known only to God leads people astray in matters of faith. Instead of guessing about details, men should leave matters of religion to God to settle through revelation.

But in 619, the ninth year of his prophethood, whatever tests the Prophet had passed were of little comfort. This would become known as the Year of Sadness, in which Muhammad lost his firmest pillars of support. The Prophet's uncle Abu Talib, chief of the Banu Hashim, died. Although he had never become Muslim, Abu Talib had protected Muhammad from his enemies and supported his mission. Now leadership of the clan passed to Abu Lahab, Muhammad's other uncle and one of the most virulent enemies of Islam. Muhammad would be sheltered no more. A month later, Muhammad's beloved wife, partner, and first follower Khadija died as well.

The Prophet was now alone, with only God to protect him. He travelled to the Arabian city of Taif to the south, hoping that its inhabitants would welcome and shelter him. Not only did the leaders of Taif reject his offer of Islam, the people pelted him with debris as he fled from the city. Gabriel appeared to Muhammad and asked him if he wanted the angels to crush Taif between two mountains. He replied, 'No, for perhaps God will cause to come from among them people who worship God alone.'

When Muhammad stopped in an orchard on his way back to Mecca, a Christian slave working amidst the trees saw him and

pitied him. He offered Muhammad some grapes, and he took them
gladly, saying 'In the name of God...' before eating. The slave
had never heard an Arab say this before, and he knew that
Muhammad had been sent by the God of the Christians.

Returning to Mecca with no one to protect him, Muhammad
called out to his tribesmen in desperation, 'Who will protect me!?'
A Quraysh noble named Mut'im bin 'Adi, despite not being
Muslim, was moved by the plight of his kinsman and offered
him his clan's protection.

Soon Muhammad was comforted by an uplifting and magnificent
experience: a mystical night journey to Jerusalem and up through
the seven heavens. One night as he slept, Gabriel appeared to
Muhammad. He beckoned him to mount a magical creature, a
white winged mule named Buraq, and voyage with him to
Jerusalem, city of his fellow prophets Solomon and David. Buraq's
strides bounded the horizon, and in moments Muhammad and
his angelic guide arrived at the Temple Mount, site of what
remained of Solomon's temple in Jerusalem. From its ruined base,
Gabriel took Muhammad up through the heavens. At every level
of the paradisaical realm, Muhammad was greeted by a prophet
from the days of yore: Jesus, Moses, even Adam, all honoured
him. In the heavenly Jerusalem, he led all the prophets in prayer.

Gabriel took him to see the splendours of paradise and the
torments of hell. Again, as when he was a child, Muhammad's
chest was split open and his heart washed in a basin full of wisdom.
As he climbed higher through the heavens, Muhammad saw a
heavenly Kaba above its earthy counterpart, and ringed around
this empyrean structure in concentric circles were thousands
upon thousands of angels each in a different position of the
Muslim prayer.

Ultimately, Muhammad was brought to the end of the created
realm, to the Furthest Lote Tree, the boundary marker between

creation and the unencompassable Creator. It is not clear what Muhammad saw – how could any mortal know?! Did he see God, or did he only see a great light through which God spoke to him as from behind a veil? Regardless, here God ordained the canonical prayer for Muslims. Until that time, Muslims had been praying twice a day, morning and night. Now they would pray together five times a day towards the holy city of Jerusalem.

Another wondrous event occurred around this time as well. One night, Muhammad absented himself from his followers to walk in the desert. The next day, Ibn Masud found him, and Muhammad told him that he had met with a group of *jinn* the night before. Ibn Masud saw their traces in the sand. These *jinn* had heard Muhammad reciting the Quran and had gone to tell their peoples about the true revelation sent down upon him by God.

After the Year of Sadness, Muhammad decided to remarry. He chose a Muslim widow from the Quraysh named Sawda, who had accompanied her late husband to refuge in Ethiopia. Soon after the wedding, Abu Bakr offered Muhammad the hand of his daughter Aisha, who is believed by historians to have been only seven years old at the time (see Chapter 2 for a discussion of Aisha's age). Muhammad had a dream in which Aisha appeared to him dressed in silken robes. An angel told the Prophet that this would be his wife in this life and the next, and he gladly accepted his good friend's offer. This would only be the marriage agreement. It would not be consummated until the girl reached puberty three years later.

Emigration and founding a new community

The city of Yathrib lay about 215 miles north of Mecca in the craggy hills of the Hejaz. It was located on more level ground than Mecca, which was situated in a steep and narrow depression amid the surrounding mountains. To the north of Yathrib was the hill of Uhud, to the south another hill, and on the east and west

Yathrib was bracketed by black, rocky lava flows – wide tracts of impassable volcanic rubble.

Between these rocky tracts, Yathrib was a collection of settlements, wells, and oases. Different clans had each built their own mud brick forts, which punctuated the rich, green date orchards (see Figure 3). Water and dates were so plentiful in Yathrib that it was said that even the horses ate dates there.

The scattered nature of the town mirrored its population. Almost half of the inhabitants belonged to three powerful Jewish tribes: the Banu Nadir, the Banu Qurayza, and the Banu Qaynuqa. Although these groups were Jewish in religion and cultivated a study of Hebrew and Aramaic, they were Arab in culture and language.

Two large pagan Arab tribes also dwelled in Yathrib, the Aws and the Khazraj. These two tribes had fallen into increasingly violent struggles in the early 600s, and the Aws had eventually gained the upper hand in a long series of skirmishes. The Jewish presence in Yathrib was influential even for these polytheist Arabs, who sometimes referred to Jewish law in their internal disputes and whose children sometimes studied in the Jewish schools.

Muhammad's mother was from Yathrib, and Khadija had relatives in the town. As a result of these connections, a small number of the Aws and the Khazraj had become Muslim. These Muslims of Yathrib thought that perhaps Muhammad could act as an outside arbitrator and bring their warring clans together. During the pilgrimage season in 621, twelve representatives of the Aws and the Khazraj Muslims met with Muhammad at a place called 'Aqaba near the pilgrimage area to pledge their allegiance to him. A year later, at the same time, a larger group came and invited Muhammad and his followers to come to Yathrib, where the Prophet would act as a chief in the town. Even though he was not Muslim, Abbas, the Prophet's paternal uncle, accompanied his nephew to advise him on his compact. The agreement between the Yathrib Muslims and Muhammad would be of momentous importance. Watching the pledge occur, Satan knew this was a great setback for his vile cause.

Muhammad soon began sending his followers to Yathrib to settle. With no family protection, just the generosity of Mut'im bin 'Adi, Muhammad and the Muslims were facing increasingly hopeless persecution in their home city. Eventually, only Muhammad, Abu Bakr, and Ali remained in Mecca. When Mut'im died in 622, Muhammad knew it was time to leave.

The Prophet was now unprotected, and the Quraysh elders gathered and agreed to send a group of men to murder Muhammad in the night. With the crime shared between all the clans, no one would be to blame. Muhammad sensed this scheme and alerted Abu Bakr to ready himself for travel. Muhammad had Ali take his place in his bed so that no one would know he had left (and also so Ali could return the goods that people had entrusted to Muhammad), and he and Abu Bakr stole out of the house. Miraculously, they were able to pass right by the group of men sent to kill the Prophet, God shielding the two refugees from their eyes. Muhammad and Abu Bakr left Mecca and struck out westwards to throw their pursuers off their track.

The famous Emigration (*Hijra*) to Yathrib had begun. With the Quraysh offering a reward of one hundred camels to whomever found the Prophet, he and Abu Bakr took refuge in a cave at nightfall. Members of the Quraysh had followed their tracks to the cave, however, and Abu Bakr warned his friend that their position was hopeless. But Muhammad replied, 'What do you think of two people when God is their third?'

Miraculously, a spider then wove an ornate web across the mouth of the small cave, and a pair of doves made their nest right by its opening. When the Quraysh drew near, although Abu

Bakr could see their feet, they did not check inside the cave. If Muhammad were hiding there, then this intricate web, which must have taken days to spin, would surely have been disturbed.

Muhammad and Abu Bakr made their way further west to the coast and then northeast towards Yathrib. As the two approached the town, Muhammad's followers welcomed him joyously. He rested for several days in the settlement of Quba on the southern end of Yathrib before mounting his favourite camel to enter Yathrib proper. The Muslims were by far the minority in the town, but they massed to meet Muhammad as he entered and sung 'The full moon has alighted upon us.' The Yathrib Muslims vied with one another to host him, but the Prophet let his camel choose a place to rest. Where she knelt down, he chose that place to build the first place of worship, or mosque, in Islam.

During the next eleven months, Muhammad stayed with a family in the town until the mosque, a rectangular enclosure with a sand courtyard partially covered by a reed awning, was complete. Muhammad would live in the spartan rooms attached to the mosque. From now on, Yathrib would be known as Medina, 'The City', short for 'The City of the Messenger of God'. Upon arriving in the city, Muhammad declared it a sacred enclave like Mecca.

Soon after arriving in Medina, Muhammad drew up a written agreement with the peoples of the town establishing relationships and obligations between the Meccan refugees, now known as 'The Immigrants' (*Muhajirun*) and the Medinan Muslims, now known as 'The Helpers' (*Ansar*). The agreement put forth articles such as 'No believer will kill another believer because of an unbeliever, and no believer will aid an unbeliever against another believer.'

Many of the smaller Jewish clans of the town were also included in this compact and were guaranteed the same security and rights as Muslims. All these groups together were 'one community'

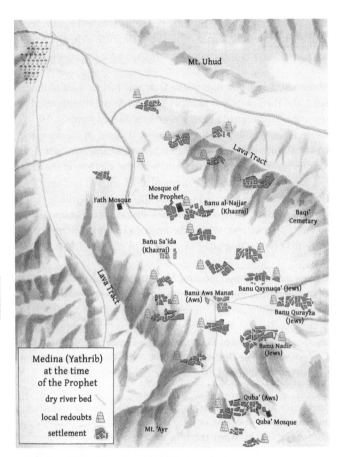

Mt. Uhud

Lava Tract

Mosque of
the Prophet

Fath Mosque

Banu al-Najjar
(Khazraj)

Baqi'
Cemetary

Banu Sa'ida
(Khazraj)

Lava Tract

Banu Qaynuqa' (Jews)

Banu Aws Manat
(Aws)

Banu Qurayza
(Jews)

Banu Nadir
(Jews)

Medina (Yathrib)
at the time
of the Prophet

dry river bed

local redoubts

settlement

Quba' (Aws)

Mt. 'Ayr

Quba' Mosque

3. Medina (Yathrib) at the time of the Prophet

(*umma*) that would make war together and peace together.
Most importantly, the document stated that 'whenever you
disagree on a matter you must refer it to God and His Messenger'.
Muhammad also struck non-aggression pacts with the three
great Jewish tribes of Medina. He was now the political and
judicial head of a city and the first Muslim community.

Within months of the migration to Medina, God revealed new rituals and duties for the Muslims. All Muslims would have to pay a charitable tax, or *zakat*, out of their personal wealth. It would be distributed amongst the poor. The month-long fast of the Arabian month of Ramadan was instituted, with no eating, drinking, or sexual activity from dawn to dusk. Muslims continued to perform their five daily prayers towards Jerusalem, but seventeen months after the migration, God revealed that Muslims would from now on pray towards the Kaba in Mecca (the direction of Muslim prayer to this day). Friday, the Medinan market day, became the day of communal prayer. Pork was forbidden. Three years later, drinking wine, already discouraged by the Quran, would also be prohibited categorically.

Yet Medina was a divided city. Within a year of Muhammad's arrival in Medina, most of the Aws and the Khazraj Arabs had become Muslim, and the number of Muslims in the town exceeded 1,500. But leading figures in those tribes harboured great resentment over the new authority wielded by Muhammad. In Mecca, anyone who claimed to be Muslim was known to be sincere – why would someone face persecution if they were not a true believer? But in Medina, a number of the Aws and the Khazraj Muslims had converted only to maintain power in the new Muslim polity. Chief among this group, whom the Quran called 'the hypocrites', was 'Abdallah bin Ubayy of the Khazraj.

There were also strong tensions between the Immigrants and the Helpers. The Meccan Immigrants had little money, having left all their property in Mecca, and they relied on the Medinan Helpers. These two groups were from totally different tribes, in addition to which the Aws and the Khazraj had themselves recently fought a war against one another. When a poet recited verses referring to the Aws/Khazraj conflict, Muhammad was forced to call out God's name to quell the resentment. In order to foster bonds of intimacy between the Helpers and the Immigrants, he created pairs of 'brothers', one from each of the two groups.

Muhammad himself, however, chose his own cousin Ali as his 'brother'.

Despite the covenant of Medina, there were also tremendous tensions between the Muslims and the Jewish tribes. The Quran called on the Jews to heed the Prophet, 'a warner from the warners of old' (Quran 53:56), whom it claimed Jewish scripture had foretold. God proclaimed:

> Say, [O Muhammad], O People of the Book! Come to a common word between us and you: that we shall worship none but God, that we shall ascribe no partner to Him, and that none of us will take each other for lords besides God.
>
> (Quran 3:64)

Although some Jews converted, like a leading rabbi of the Banu Qaynuqa, 'Abdallah bin Salam, the majority resisted Muhammad's call. Sometimes Jews even mocked the Prophet. When Muhammad lost some of his camels, some Jews laughed at the notion that this man claimed to receive revelations from God but could not even find his own livestock. The Jews continued to test Muhammad, asking him what the proper Abrahamic punishment for adultery was (stoning, Muhammad replied) and inquiring as to who created God. The Quran replied definitively in a short chapter that rebutted Christian beliefs as well: 'Say He is the One God, the All Sought After, He does not beget nor is He begotten, and there is none like unto Him' (Quran 112:1–4).

War with Mecca and a miraculous victory

For Muhammad and his followers, especially the Meccan Immigrants, all thoughts turned quickly to their families in Mecca, to regaining their lost property, and one day their home. Always commanding the Muslims to turn the other cheek when they were in Mecca, God now allowed them to stand up for their rights:

Permission has been given to those who fight because they have been wronged. Indeed God is most able to give them succour; those who were driven from their homes unjustly, for but saying 'Our lord is God'. And if God did not repel one group of people with another, monasteries, temples and places of kneeling where God's name is mentioned would be destroyed.

(Quran 22:39–40)

The Muslims soon began raiding Meccan caravans, and Muhammad began pursuing alliances with other Arab tribes, both Muslim and pagan.

In 624, two years after the migration, Muhammad led a detachment of Muslims, mostly Immigrants, to seize a large Meccan caravan led by Abu Sufyan as it returned from Syria. But when they had learned that their most prized caravan of the year was under threat, the Quraysh leadership of Abu Jahl, Walid, Umayya bin Khalaf (the man who had tortured Bilal with rocks), and others had led a massive army to protect it and eliminate the threat that the Muslims presented to the caravan route.

Muhammad and the Muslims were now faced with an unforeseen challenge: approximately 300 Muslims were facing a Meccan army three times that size. The Prophet adopted the strategy suggested by one of his Companions: seize the wells at a settlement by the plain of Badr so that the Quraysh could not access the water. The Muslims then made camp and prepared to confront the Meccans at dawn.

The next day, in mid-March 624, the outnumbered Muslim army faced the Meccan forces. Following custom, each side sent out champions to face one another in single combat. Muhammad sent out three men, including Ali, already a feared warrior, and his uncle Hamza. They faced three leading men of the Quraysh, including 'Utba bin Rabi'a and al-Walid bin 'Utba. Within a few minutes, both Walid and 'Utba, two of the fiercest enemies of Islam, lay dead at Ali's and Hamza's hands. In the melee that ensued, some 70 Meccans were killed and only 15 Muslims died. Among the Quraysh dead lay two more archenemies of Muhammad: Abu Jahl and Umayya. The Quraysh retreated, shocked and defeated.

The Muslim victory was nothing short of miraculous. Bedouins who had witnessed the battle from hills above recalled seeing angelic figures in the clouds aiding the Muslims. The Quran told the Muslims 'It was not you who hurled [your spears] when you hurled them, but God' (Quran 8:17). Islam was no longer a contemptible nuisance in Arabia. It was a force to be reckoned with. The Quraysh leadership had been decimated in one battle against a vastly smaller force. As Hassan bin Thabit, the Prophet's chief poet, sang of the Battle of Badr:

> So how many a noble and generous man we killed,
> Renowned and revered amongst his tribe.

With almost 70 prominent Quraysh prisoners, Muhammad was faced with the choice of executing them or ransoming them back to their families. Umar, now a close lieutenant of Muhammad, urged him to kill these known enemies of Islam, since they would simply return to fight the Muslims again if allowed to live. Muhammad, however, decided to ransom them, although he freed those captives who embraced Islam. One of the prisoners at Badr was the Prophet's uncle Abbas, whom the Prophet had ordered his soldiers not to kill in battle because he had been coerced into fighting against the Muslims. The Prophet could not sleep he was so tormented that his uncle was in fetters, so he ordered him released. Abbas told the Prophet in secret that he had been Muslim for some time but had not declared it openly. Muhammad replied, 'God knows best about your being Muslim, if what you say is true then God will reward you.' Later, God revealed that Umar had been right: 'It is not for a prophet to

take prisoners until he has established himself in the land'
(Quran 8:67).

As the Muslim army was returning victorious to Medina,
however, they were met by tragic news. Muhammad's daughter
and the wife of Uthman, Ruqayya, had died of an illness during
the battle. Uthman would soon remarry – another of Muhammad's
daughters, Umm Kulthum. For this reason, Uthman was known
as 'He of the Two Lights'.

Death struck in Mecca as well. Abu Lahab was so frustrated by
the defeat at Badr that he began beating one of Abbas' Muslim
slaves. Abbas' wife, Umm Fadl, who was herself Muslim, picked up
a tent pole and smashed Abu Lahab on the head. His wound
festered and he died several days later in repulsive agony.

Medina resounded with celebrations in praise of God after the
great victory of what became known as the Battle of Badr. What
more proof did the Muslims need that God favoured them? But
soon division struck. A Muslim woman was visiting the
settlement of the Banu Qaynuqa Jews where the Medinan gold
market was located. A Jew pinned her dress to the bench on which
she was seated so when she stood up her rear end was bared to
all. Much laughter ensued. A Muslim leapt on the Jewish
merchant to avenge the woman's honour and killed him; the
Jews killed the Muslim in return. When Muhammad demanded
that the Banu Qaynuqa appear before him to settle the matter
by arbitration, they refused.

Sensing an imminent conflict, the Jews fortified themselves in
their bastions with the assistance of some of the Muslim
hypocrites. When the Muslims besieged them, the Banu Qaynuqa
agreed to exile and went north to join the Jewish tribes in the
oasis cities of Tayma' and Khaybar. As a lesson from this episode,
the Quran warned Muslims not to take Jews or Christians as
friends and allies in opposition to other Muslims.

Near defeat and pensiveness

Eager to avenge the Meccan dead, Abu Sufyan, now the senior leader of the Quraysh, mustered a large army of 3,000 men and 200 cavalry and moved against Medina in 625 (about a year after the Battle of Badr). Muhammad initially wanted to remain in Medina and prepare to withstand a siege, but the veterans of Badr, confident of divine support, urged him to ride out and meet the Meccans where they had camped by the hill of Uhud three miles north of Medina.

The Muslims numbered about 1,000 men, but at the last minute the hypocrite 'Abdallah bin Ubayy deserted Muhammad with 300 of his men. Nevertheless, with their backs to the hill and God in their hearts, the Muslims began a rout of the Meccans. But the Muslim archers, whom Muhammad had positioned at the rear to protect the infantry, were overcome by greed for spoils of war and left their stations.

The young Quraysh lieutenant Khalid bin al-Walid exploited this gap in the Muslim line and led the Meccan cavalry to encircle the stunned Muslims. Muhammad and his Companions retreated up the hill, but in the fray Muhammad himself was wounded: a sword blow to his helmet cut his cheek, another bruised his arm, and a stone from a sling knocked out one of his teeth. Some of the Muslims believed Muhammad had been killed and despaired. Even when wounded, however, Muhammad did not cease fighting and aiding his Companions. One Muslim's eye was injured so badly that it hung out on his cheek. Muhammad miraculously healed the eye by placing it back in its socket.

Amidst the turmoil, the Muslim forces were struck a great blow: Hamza was killed. Hind, the wife of Abu Sufyan and daughter of the 'Utba bin Rabi'a whom Hamza had killed at Badr in single combat, orchestrated his death. She paid a slave named Wahshi, who was known for his prowess with the javelin, to hunt down and kill Hamza on the battlefield. After the battle, Hind mutilated Hamza's face and body and ate part of his liver.

Despite Muhammad's shocking wounds and Hamza's death, the Muslims were able to retreat and avoid a full-scale defeat. Many of the Muslims who carried the flag of Islam that day fell protecting it. One man, an Ethiopian slave, held the standard aloft until his arms were cut off. Holding the flag between his chin and chest, he was struck down at last.

Sixty-five Muslims died that day, compared to only twenty-two unbelievers. Fortunately, one of the Meccans' allies was secretly in alliance with Muhammad. Though himself not a Muslim, this chief managed to convince Abu Sufyan not to press home his advantage and crush the Muslims once and for all.

The Muslims were terribly disillusioned by their near rout at the Battle of Uhud, as it was called. Clearly, God had tested them to see who was truly a devout follower of Islam. The desertion of the hypocrites and the allure of greed had demonstrated the weak faith of the community, the essentiality of trust in God, and the human origin of defeat. As God revealed after the battle, 'If some great calamity afflicts you (you have afflicted it twice fold), do you say, "How can this be?" Say: "It is from your own selves"' (Quran 3:165). God also revealed why He tests men: 'These days, we award them to the people in turns so that God might know which amongst you believes, and so that He might take martyrs from among you' (Quran 3:140).

The Muslims were also faced with the distinction between their beloved Prophet and the religion he preached. The notion of Muhammad's death was almost inconceivable to them. But God reminded the Muslims that Islam was greater than Muhammad: 'Muhammad is no more than a messenger: many were the messengers that passed away before him. If he died or were killed, would you then turn on your heels?' (Quran 3:144).

The Prophet ordered the dead of Uhud to be buried unwashed on the battlefield. Such was his haste to retreat and seek security. Later, during the rule of the Umayyad caliphs, a canal was dug to bring water to Medina, and these martyrs were disinterred. Their bodies had not decayed at all.

As the Muslims searched their souls after the near defeat, trouble again arose with the Medinan Jews. A man from one of the smaller Jewish clans had killed a Muslim, and Muhammad went to visit the Banu Nadir Jews to receive some of the compensation money from them. Members of the Banu Nadir conspired, however, to drop a rock on Muhammad from their redoubt. Muhammad was made aware of the scheme, however, and ordered a siege of the Banu Nadir forts. When he threatened to cut down their date palms, the Banu Nadir agreed to exile. They were allowed to take whatever property they could carry, and they went north to the oasis of Khaybar. Two Jews who decided to become Muslim were allowed to stay and retain their property. Muhammad distributed what remained of the Banu Nadir's wealth amongst the Immigrants and poor Helpers.

Muhammad: the Beloved of God and goodly example

One Muslim woman in Medina lost her father, husband, and brother in the Battle of Uhud. Yet when the army returned from the field, she broke into tears of joyous relief to see the Prophet alive and well. She had boundless love for the man whom God had singled out with His words: 'Indeed God and His angels send mercy down upon the Prophet. O you who believe, send your blessings and bountiful peace upon him!' (Quran 33:56).

To his followers, Muhammad was 'The Messenger of God and the Seal of the Prophets' (Quran 33:40). He was the font of blessings and sole point of contact with the divine. God commanded the Muslims to obey His Messenger Muhammad, for he was 'possessed of an awesome character' and 'a goodly exemplar' for the Muslims (Quran 68:4, 33:21). Muhammad's teachings, words, and behaviour were a living implementation and illustration of the Quran's teachings. As his wife Aisha said, 'His character *was* the Quran.' Muhammad's precedent and the totality of his lifestyle became known as his Sunnah, which Muslims believed was inspired by God – a veritable second revelation. As Muhammad once said, 'I was given the Quran and its like along with it.'

Who was this leader whom the Muslims loved so dearly that they prized him above their own parents and children? Who was this man whom they venerated so clearly that they imitated his every action, how he ate, slept, and dressed (later people would remark to the Muslims that 'your prophet has taught you everything, even how to defecate')?

Muhammad was of medium height and build, with olive skin and shoulder-length, jet-black hair, which he often wore in two braids. He had a beard long enough that it could be seen upon his cheeks from behind him, and he had a slight gap between his top front teeth. He owned only two pairs of clothing, long blouses pulled on over the head, and a cloak to protect him from the cold. Although he was often presented with ornate robes as gifts, he gave them away to his followers. Like everyone in the desert, the Prophet covered his head with a turban, either black or green. He wore a simple ring with the inscription 'Muhammad the Messenger of God'. Like his Arab people, he wore kohl around his eyes.

It was Muhammad who taught the Muslims how to perform their five daily prayers, when to begin and end their fasts, and how to undertake the various rites of pilgrimage to Mecca. In such rituals and practices, Muhammad preferred to adhere to the ways of the People of the Book unless God ordered some change. His Companions followed the Sunnah obsessively. Later, when Umar bin al-Khattab was leading the Muslims in their circumambulation of the Kaba, he stopped to kiss the black stone as Muhammad had taught him. 'I know you are but a rock that cannot hurt or harm me', he scoffed at the stone, 'and I would not kiss you if I had not seen this done by the Messenger of God.'

In Muslim tradition, the devotion that Muslims should feel towards Muhammad is seen as a reflection of the magnanimity of his character. Even Abu Sufyan could only admit that 'I have never seen someone who was as loved as Muhammad was by his Companions.' To be near him, to hear him speak, was to draw near to the bridge between the divine and the earthly realm. Muhammad's person was so imbued with *baraka*, or blessing, that to touch him felt like brief contact with God's grace. Companions would fight over the water left over from Muhammad's ablutions, collect his hairs and fingernail clippings. 'Abdallah bin al-Zubayr, the first Muslim born in Medina, once even tasted some of the Prophet's blood after he had been bled when sick.

Muhammad was infinitely wise, always aware of the virtuous course of action as a father, a friend, a judge, and a leader of men. 'I have been sent', he said, 'to complete the virtues of character.' He said that God had granted him 'encompassing words (*jawami' al-kalam*)', or the ability to speak profound truths succinctly. 'The best of affairs are those of moderation', he said one day; 'Happy is the man who heeds the lessons learned by others', he said on another.

Arabs respected courage and wise council, and Muhammad exemplified both. He fought in nine battles during his career, always sharing the risks taken by his men. But he also knew the central importance of alliances, even with unbelievers.

His mercy and patience were inexhaustible. When a coarse Bedouin came to Medina from the desert and began relieving himself in the mosque courtyard, Muhammad's Companions wanted to kill him for his disrespect. Muhammad told them to let the man finish. He then told the Bedouin, 'The mosque is for praying.' When he was injured at Uhud, the Muslims urged Muhammad to curse the Meccans. He replied, 'Truly I was not sent to curse, but rather to call people to religion and as a mercy. O God! They are my people, but they know not.'

Muhammad was incredibly charitable in his judgement of other Muslims' sincerity. His close Companion Usama bin Zayd killed a man in battle despite the fact that right before he swung his sword the man had cried out 'There is no deity but God, and Muhammad is His messenger' – presumably becoming Muslim to save his skin. But the Prophet rebuked Usama: 'Did you split open his heart [to know what he truly believed]?', Muhammad asked.

Muhammad was exceptionally frugal and pious. He never ate his fill of bread or meat without sharing it with others. 'Food for one will suffice for two', he said, 'and food for two will suffice for three'. When Aisha was asked how he acted at home, she said, 'He was a man like any other, he would delouse his clothing, milk his own sheep and tend to his own needs.'

Muhammad always mentioned God in his every action. When he ate, he would pray, for example, 'Praise be to God who feeds us and gives us drink and has made us among those who submit to Him.' He prayed for at least a third of every night, and fasted every Monday and Thursday. This despite the fact that God had revealed to him that he was guaranteed paradise. When a Muslim asked Muhammad why he continued to worship and fast so frequently, Muhammad replied, 'Should I not be a grateful servant of God?' But Muhammad was attentive that he did not set too difficult a standard for his followers; in any new situation, he would always take the easiest option if it was not a sin.

The fear of God and concern for his community weighed heavily upon Muhammad, but he was a man of exceptional good humour. One of his Companions said that he had 'never seen anyone smile as much as the Messenger of God'. Although he instructed his followers, 'Do not lie even if you're joking', Muhammad was not above a hearty laugh. When Ali had a spat with his wife, Muhammad's daughter Fatima, and fell asleep outside his house in the dust, Muhammad named him Abu Turab, the 'Father of Dust', a nickname that stuck.

Muhammad never spared himself criticism. A man who was riding next to the Prophet during a campaign accidentally struck Muhammad's foot, and the pain led Muhammad to strike the man's leg with his whip. The next day, the Prophet sought the man out to apologize and compensate him with eighty camels. But if Muhammad felt that someone was belittling him in his capacity as God's Messenger, he was uncompromising in his response. When a man accused Muhammad of nepotism when he ruled in favour of his cousin al-Zubayr in a matter of splitting irrigation water, Muhammad stripped the man of all his water rights.

Muhammad's authority amongst the Muslims was two-fold: that of a political leader and that of a religious guide. Although Muhammad was ultimately the decision-maker in Medina's political and judicial affairs, as we have seen, he consulted with his advisors such as Umar and frequently yielded to their council.

As a religious leader, however, Muhammad brooked no dissent. To break with his delivery of God's message and definition of Islam was to leave the Muslim community – the testimony of faith said to become a Muslim was 'There is no deity but God, and Muhammad is the messenger of God.' A Medinan man named Abu Amir had been a *hanif* following the religion of Abraham before Muhammad's arrival in the city. But Abu Amir accused Muhammad of adulterating the Abrahamic faith, to which Muhammad replied, 'No, I have renewed it pure and white.' As a result, Abu Amir was exiled from Medina and eventually joined the Meccans. The Quran reminded the Muslims that 'It is not for a believing man or woman that they should have any choice in a matter when God and His Messenger have decided it' (Quran 33:36).

Insulting or attacking the person of the Prophet was an attack on the core of Islam and Muslim identity. Within Medina, Muhammad was merciful. After the Prophet was wounded at Uhud, the arch-hypocrite 'Abdallah bin Ubayy had claimed that no true prophet could be injured in battle. When Umar and other Companions wanted to kill the hypocrite for his calumny, Muhammad responded that he did not want anyone to say that Muhammad kills his own Companions. Even the Jews who mocked the Prophet within Medina were left unmolested.

Satirical poetry, however, was a political weapon. In Arabia, poets were the propagandists in times of conflict. A Medinan poet named Ka'b al-Ashraf joined the Meccans after the Battle of Badr and later composed vicious satires of Muhammad. Muhammad ordered his followers to find and assassinate him. Later, the Prophet also ordered the assassination of a female poet from a desert tribe who was slandering him in verse.

A siege and an execution

Abu Sufyan and the Meccan elite regretted not deracinating Islam when they had the chance, and they began building a massive army of allies to annihilate the Muslims once and for all. In 627, a 10,000-man allied army made up mostly of the Quraysh, warriors from the powerful tribe of Ghatafan (a tribe which the Muslims had raided earlier), and other smaller groups including elements of the Jewish Banu Nadir tribe, converged on Medina.

Muhammad consulted his Companions on the best course of action. The solution came from Salman al-Farisi, a Persian who had migrated to Arabia. In Iran, Salman said, they would dig trenches around their cities to defend against cavalry attacks. 'Warfare is deception', commented Muhammad.

Medina was well guarded on three sides by hills and the lava flow – all the Muslims needed to do was dig a trench to protect the city's exposed northwestern face. Muhammad approved of the plan, and the Muslims commenced digging immediately. When a group of workers struck an immovable rock, they called Muhammad to help them break it. On the first blow of his axe, a light flashed in the direction of Syria; on the second, a light flashed south towards Yemen. On the third blow, the rock splintered, sending a shaft of light in the direction of Sassanian Persia. Salman knew this was a portent, and Muhammed explained that it foretold the conquest of these kingdoms by Islam.

During the toil of digging, a Muslim woman brought a tray of dates for Muhammad. But the Prophet would not eat them alone. He invited all the workers to partake, and the small tray miraculously filled and refilled to satiate all the workers' hunger. The trench was dug in six days, just in time to stop the allied army in its tracks. The allied cavalry could not cross the trench, and the infantry was held back by the Muslim defenders. The Battle of the Ditch had begun.

For two weeks, the allied army besieged Medina, occasionally succeeding in sending small detachments of troops across the trench. Ali led the Muslim counter-offensives, in one battle killing the most vaunted Meccan warrior. The Prophet noted that it was the most severe combat he had ever witnessed. The Banu Qurayza Jews, whose compounds lay outside the defences of the town, broke their treaty with Muhammad and sold provisions to the Meccans.

As the siege wore on, however, the Meccan alliance began to crumble. The leader of Ghatafan offered a secret truce to

Muhammad: peace in return for half of Medina's date crop the next year. Muhammad was inclined to accept, but his Companions strongly objected, and he refused. Finally, the Meccan alliance, poorly provisioned and weary, dissolved. Muhammad and the Muslims were triumphant, for they had survived the most concerted attempt yet to destroy Islam. From that day onwards, Muslims would be on the offensive.

But first Muhammad faced the question of the Banu Qurayza Jews. They had betrayed their non-aggression pact with the Muslims, and as the Meccan army left, they blockaded themselves in their forts and prepared for a Muslim siege. Muhammad offered them the choice of converting to Islam, but all but a handful refused. Realizing they could not lift the Muslim siege, the Jews surrendered. Muhammad allowed the chief of the Aws tribe, who had been closely allied with the Banu Qurayza before, to determine their punishment. He decided that the men should be executed and the women and children sold into slavery.

In April of 627, some 400 men of the Banu Qurayza were executed by the sword (their leader, who had condemned siding with the Meccans, and those few who converted to Islam were spared). Approximately 1,000 women and children were sold to the tribes of Najd in return for arms and provisions. Muhammad took one woman, Rayhana, for his concubine, and she later converted to Islam.

The miracles of the Prophet

When the Quraysh had asked Muhammad for some sign of his prophecy, like an angel descending visibly upon them with a tangible revealed tablet, the Quran had replied that God only sends humans as messengers (17:90-6). It is God's message which proves its own truth. What good do miracles really do, after all? Had the followers of Moses not turned their backs on him even after God had parted the Red Sea? Muhammad was but a mortal messenger. As the Quran instructed him to say, 'I tell you not that with me are the treasures of God, that I know what is hidden, nor do I tell you that I am an angel. I do but follow what is revealed to me' (Quran 6:50).

The Quran presents itself, with its peerless beauty and consistency, as the ultimate proof of Muhammad's prophethood: 'Do they not ponder the Quran? Had it come from other than God, surely they would have found in it much discrepancy' (Quran 4:82). God challenges the unbelievers to produce even one chapter like the Quran, a challenge they never took up.

But God supported Muhammad and his followers with miraculous signs and assistance throughout his prophetic career. In Mecca, God protected Muhammad from physical harm on numerous occasions. Once Abu Jahl had fumed, 'O men of Quraysh, indeed this Muhammad, how he has slandered our religion, cursed our fathers, mocked our dreams, and insulted our gods!' and decided to murder Muhammad. The next day, when Abu Jahl stole up behind the Prophet ready to crush his skull with a rock, a great camel stallion, foaming at the mouth and mad, came between the Prophet and his attacker and frightened Abu Jahl away. Later, Muhammad would tell his followers that it was Gabriel who had taken a camel's form.

In Mecca, God produced the greatest and most miraculous proof of Muhammad's prophethood. Acceding to the Quraysh's demand for a sign, God split the moon at Muhammad's request, and its two halves hung above the mountains. 'Bear witness!' Muhammad called out. Still sceptical, the Quraysh questioned travellers who arrived days later if they had witnessed the wonder. Indeed, they had. As the Quran revealed, 'The Hour has drawn near and the moon has split asunder' (Quran 54:1).

Miracles accompanied the Prophet in Medina as well. Before his mosque was built, Muhammad had delivered his sermons for the

Friday communal prayer leaning against a palm stump. When his mosque was completed and a pulpit installed, people regularly heard the stump moaning in longing for the Prophet's touch. At a market in Medina, some 300 of Muhammad's Companions needed water to perform their ablutions for prayer. Muhammad called for a bucket of water and placed his hand in it. Suddenly, water began to flow from between his fingers, enough for all his followers to use.

Such miracles drew many into the fold of Islam. On a raid against the Ghatafan tribe, Muhammad had withdrawn from the army to rest against a tree. A member of the Ghatafan named Du'thur snuck up unnoticed, and Muhammad awoke suddenly to find the man standing above him with a drawn sword. 'Are you not afraid?' Du'thur asked, shocked by Muhammad's calm. 'God will suffice me', the Prophet answered, and Du'thur was struck with a back pain so severe that he dropped his sword and crumpled to the ground. Muhammad picked up the sword, and Du'thur, wonderstruck, embraced Islam that instant.

Treaties and strategy

The year after the Battle of the Ditch, in 628 CE, God inspired Muhammad to prepare for a pilgrimage. It was during one of the Arabian sacred months, when fighting was prohibited. Muhammad ordered his followers to prepare for the lesser pilgrimage, which could be performed separately from the great *Hajj*, and pay homage to the House of God in the lion's den of Mecca. It is not clear exactly how many, but between 700 and 1,400 men accompanied the Prophet wearing the pilgrim's garb of two white cloths and leading the sacrificial camels which would be slaughtered ritually in Mecca. They also tucked swords into their saddles, aware of the danger they might face. They proceeded solemnly towards Mecca, chanting the traditional pilgrimage call: 'Here I am at your service, O God!'

When the Muslims reached a resting place known as Hudaybiyya on the edge of the sacred territory around Mecca, Muhammad sent Uthman, a kinsman of Abu Sufyan, ahead to warn the Meccans of the Muslims' peaceful intentions. The Quraysh, however, faced an unenviable predicament. As the custodians of the sacred sanctuary, their reputation rested on openly hosting all those who wished to visit the Kaba shrine. But if they allowed Muhammad and the Muslims to perform their pilgrimage, this would legitimize their upstart religion in the eyes of all.

Suddenly, Muhammad was seized with the same transfixed state that accompanied the revelation of the Quran, and he asked the Muslims to come to him and pledge their renewed allegiance to him. As the Prophet sat beneath a blooming acacia tree, all but one of the Muslims came forward to swear an oath of allegiance, and Muhammad himself pledged for the absent Uthman.

The Meccans sent envoys, and together they reached a settlement with Muhammad. The Muslims would return home to Medina that year, but the next year they could perform the great pilgrimage and reside safely in Mecca for three days. Moreover, there would be peace between Mecca and Medina for ten years, during which time both sides could strike up whatever alliances they saw fit. If a Meccan wanted to immigrate to Medina and join the Muslim community without the permission of his parent or guardian, however, Muhammad would have to turn him away.

Tragically, just as this agreement was solidified, the figure of Abu Jandal, a Meccan Muslim long imprisoned by his father, appeared out of the desert. He had escaped Mecca, but, as dictated by the newly signed Treaty of Hudaybiyya, Muhammad returned him to Mecca. Umar was angry and confused with Muhammad's decision, and even Muhammad's explanation that God's wisdom transcended all did not assuage him. Abu Bakr tried to calm Umar too, and later the gruff lieutenant begged the Prophet's forgiveness.

As they left Hudaybiyya to return to Medina, the Quran comforted both Umar and the Prophet: 'Indeed We have granted you a manifest victory.' The Quran continued, 'God was well pleased with the believers when they pledged their allegiance to you under the tree. Thus He knew what was in their hearts and bestowed tranquillity upon them, and rewarded them with a victory near at hand' (Quran 48:1, 18). The magnitude of this victory was beyond the Muslims' imagination at that time, although in the two years after Hudaybiyya the Muslim community doubled in size through peacetime conversion.

Although the Medinan community was at peace with Mecca, Muhammad continued to build alliances with neighbouring tribes. Muhammad's strategic thinking was international in scope. He sent letters and emissaries to the Sassanian king of Persia inviting him to Islam. The Persian governor of Yemen converted to Islam in 628, handing his province over to Muslim rule. Muhammad sent calls to Islam to the Byzantine governor of Alexandria in Egypt, and the heads of the great Arab tribes who served as border guards for the Sassanians in southern Iraq and for the Byzantines in Syria.

Muhammad sent his Companion Dihya to meet with the Byzantine emperor Heraclius himself, who was in Syria after his victory there over the Persians. Muhammad's letter called Heraclius to embrace Islam and not to forsake Muhammad as the disciples of Jesus had forsaken him and his message. Heraclius sent a letter to his most accomplished religious scholar in Constantinople, and he replied that Muhammad was 'the Most Praised (Ahmad)' that the Bible had foretold. However, when Heraclius informed his generals of his decision to embrace Islam, they nearly revolted, and he recanted quickly (remember, this is a sacred history, for analysis see Chapter 2).

The Jews of the Hejaz and more campaigns

With a peace treaty with Mecca secured, Muhammad turned his mind to the town of Khaybar, which lay in the mountains of the

Hejaz some 95 miles north of Medina. The city was populated by Jewish tribes, including the exiled Banu Nadir, who had played a crucial role in cementing the alliance which besieged Medina during the Battle of the Ditch. As alluring as settling the score with these enemies was the agricultural wealth of Khaybar, which was famous for its rich date farms and crafts. In late May of 628, Muhammad marched to Khaybar at the head of an army of 1,700 infantry and 200 cavalry. He promised that the bulk of the spoils they captured would go to those Muslims who had pledged their allegiance to him at Hudaybiyya.

The Muslims caught the Jews of Khaybar unaware, and after a brief but vicious battle on the open plain, the Jewish forces retired into the mudbrick redoubts that dotted the date orchards of the town. At one particularly stubborn keep, the senior Companions urged the Muslim troops forward against the walls of the citadel. First Abu Bakr took the Muslim standard, then Umar, and then finally the renowned young warrior Ali. He had been suffering from an eye infection, but the Prophet spit in his eye and it was miraculously cured. In an unmatched display of valour, Ali tore the door off the fort and used it as his great shield, eventually crashing his sword down on the head of the Jewish chief so that his helmet, head, and upper body were split in half.

Finally, the Jews of Khaybar agreed to a negotiated truce: they could remain in Khaybar if they paid half their annual date yield to the Muslims in tribute. As the Quran dictated, Muhammad took one-fifth of the land of Khaybar as his to distribute to his wives, family, and others he deemed fit.

The Muslim armies subdued the other Jewish oases of the Hejaz as well. The town of Tayma', for example, surrendered peacefully, and agreed to pay the *jizya*, or a tax levied on non-Muslims to retain their right to practise their religion and enjoy the protection of the Muslim army. While eating a dinner hosted by a Jewish family of Khaybar, however, a Jewish woman poisoned the lamb shoulder that was being served to Muhammad and his aides. Muhammad heard the meat telling him it was poisoned, and he stopped eating it. One of his Companions had eaten too much, however, and died. The poison that Muhammad had ingested made him ill for a time, and until his death he sometimes felt pangs of pain from the poison.

Marriages, alliances, and the home front

Exactly how many wives Muhammad had after his beloved Khadija died was widely researched by Muslim scholars, but some details remain unclear. Ibn Hisham (d. 833), the Egyptian scholar whose edition of the Prophet's biography is most famous, concluded that Muhammad married thirteen women in all, consummated his marriage with eleven of them (two he divorced before consummation), and was married to at most nine at one time. He also had two concubines.

In addition to Sawda and Aisha, Muhammad married the daughter of another of his close aides: Hafsa, the daughter of Umar ibn al-Khattab. Hafsa was the widow of a Muslim who died at Badr, and she later played an important role in the official collection and compilation of the Quran. Muhammad married another divorcee, Umm Habiba, whose husband had converted to Christianity while the two were refugees in Ethiopia. Ironically, Umm Habiba was the daughter of Abu Sufyan, having embraced the faith that her father so reviled. A woman named Umm Salama, whose husband and father of her four children was killed at the Battle of Uhud, soon thereafter also became a wife of Muhammad. Near the end of his life, Muhammad also married the double-divorcee Maymuna bint al-Harith, the sister-in-law of his uncle Abbas.

The Prophet married a Jewish noblewoman as well. Safiyya was the daughter of a chief of the Banu Nadir who had settled in Khaybar. She was taken prisoner after the battle, and Muhammad freed and married her. Even after Safiyya converted to Islam, she was sometimes treated coldly by Muhammad's other wives. Umm Salama once refused to lend her a camel when Safiyya's had gone lame, saying 'What?! Am I to lend something to this Jewess!?' When Safiyya complained to the Prophet of such treatment, he told her to tell his other wives that she was the daughter of a rabbi and thus, 'My father was Aaron and my uncle Moses.'

Muhammad also married a number of women to cement tribal alliances. He wed Juwayriyya bint al-Harith, a widow who was the daughter of the chief of the powerful Banu Mustaliq clan of the Khuza'a tribe, against whom the Muslims had warred. He also married a woman from the Banu 'Amir bin Sa'sa'a, whose name is unknown, as well as a woman from the great Kinda tribe of Najd. This last wife asked Muhammad to grant her a divorce so that she might return to her people, and he acceded.

The Prophet had one very controversial marriage: his union with Zaynab bint Jahsh, the former wife of his adopted son Zayd. So problematic was this relationship that the Quran itself instructed the Prophet on the proper course of action, and Zayd is one of only two contemporaries of Muhammad ever mentioned by name in the holy book.

Muhammad had overseen the marriage between Zayd and Zaynab, who was known for her beauty. When the couple began having problems, Muhammad encouraged them to remain together. But the nature of the problem was particularly sensitive: Zaynab was in love with the Prophet. Ultimately, Muhammad accepted the divorce and, soon after, married Zaynab.

Rumours flew. Had Muhammad desired Zaynab all along? It was rumoured that he had once accidentally seen her changing and become infatuated. But these rumours were not the heart of the controversy. In Arabia, like the rest of the ancient Near East, an adopted son was essentially a real son in every sense. To marry

Zaynab after Zayd, who was known as 'Zayd the son of Muhammad', would mean that the Prophet was marrying his son's former wife – an act strictly prohibited by the Quran and considered repulsive by Arabs. But the Quran revealed that adopted sons were *not* like real sons at all, and they should never even take their fathers' family names. There was therefore no problem with Muhammad marrying Zaynab. What had started as a controversy, Muslims thus understood, became a lesson from God on the correct nature of adoption.

The wives of the Prophet each lived in a room off the main courtyard of the Medina mosque. With their lives so open to the public, after the Battle of the Ditch the Quran ordered the wives of the Prophet to separate themselves from the general public by a veil or curtain. Muhammad himself had no private rooms. He would take regular turns living with each of his wives. In addition, he would visit each one every day.

In addition to his wives, Muhammad had two concubines: Rayhana and Marya, a Coptic slave woman who had been sent by the governor of Alexandria as a present to the Prophet. The Prophet became very fond of Marya, and he built a small house for her away from the mosque. His wives, however, became jealous of the attention he paid her and demanded that he stop seeing her. Muhammad agreed reluctantly, but the Quran reminded him that he was not to prohibit for himself what God had made licit and reprimanded his wives (Quran 66:1–5).

Muhammad's wives occasionally feuded with him and with one another. Once, Aisha even knocked over a dish of food that a fellow wife was offering to the Prophet and threw its contents at her. At one point, Muhammad's wives collectively asked for more luxury and wealth. So saddened was Muhammad by this request that he withdrew from his wives for almost two months. Umar advised the Prophet to divorce his wives (even though his own daughter was among them), and the Quran reminded the wives that God could easily replace them with others more worthy. God ordered Muhammad to give them a choice: if they wanted material wealth, God would give it to them. But if they 'desired God and His Messenger and the Hereafter, then surely God has prepared for those who do good among you a great reward' (Quran 33:29). Muhammad's wives all pleaded for forgiveness, and the Quran then honoured them with the title 'the Mothers of the Believers'.

Muhammad, however, had no children from any of his wives after the children born by Khadija. Marya bore him a son, named Ibrahim (Abraham), but he died in infancy.

The greatest challenge that Muhammad faced on the home front was the infamous affair of 'The Lie'. On the way back from a campaign, Aisha had descended from her camel litter to look for a necklace that had fallen in the sand. The caravan departed without knowing that she was gone. The distraught young woman was rescued by a young Muslim who had fallen behind the main body of the army. He then returned Aisha safely to the Prophet.

In Arabia, however, for a woman to be alone with a strange man was a severe threat to her honour. A number of Muslims began spreading rumours that the two young travellers had been unable to resist one another. Among those circulating the rumour was one of Zaynab's cousins and the Prophet's favourite poet Hassan bin Thabit.

Muhammad was embarrassed and concerned. Were the rumours true? Could he trust his wife? Ali advised him that there were other women he could marry besides Aisha, 'Women are plentiful, and you can easily change one for another.' A month passed, during which time Aisha pled her innocence and Muhammad waited for some exculpatory sign. Finally, God revealed a verse of the Quran vindicating Aisha and condemning the slanderers.

Those who had spread the vile rumour were punished with eighty lashes, the Quranic ruling for calumny.

The crumbling of Quraysh and the conquest of Mecca

During the peace of Hudaybiyya, the number of tribes who embraced Islam and allied themselves with Medina grew substantially. The more perspicacious Meccans knew that the future belonged to the Messenger of God. 'Amr bin al-'As, well known to be the craftiest young man of the Quraysh, had converted to Islam at the hands of the Negus in Ethiopia while attempting to convince the king to expel the Muslim refugees. Khalid, the young man of Makhzum who had almost routed the Muslims at Uhud, learned that his own mother had become Muslim. Speaking to 'Amr, he observed that the plight of Quraysh was like that of a fox in a hole – if you pour water in, it must eventually come out. In the eighth year after the *Hijra*, both Khalid and 'Amr made the voyage to Medina to enter Islam. 'Amr's political genius and Khalid's military prowess would soon become legendary as Islam spread beyond Arabia. The Prophet himself would dub Khalid 'the Drawn Sword of Islam'.

The truce of Hudaybiyya would not hold for long. So numerous were the varied tribes allied either to the Meccans or Medina that eventually some conflict between these two blocks was inevitable. When Meccan allies attacked associates of Medina, Muhammad leapt on the chance to deal a fatal blow to his enemies.

In 630 CE, the Prophet led a massive army of 10,000 Muslims towards Mecca. On the way to the city, the army came across the Prophet's uncle Abbas, who had started his emigration to Medina to follow Islam openly. As the Muslim army made its camp outside Mecca, the Quraysh knew that this potent a force could not be resisted. Abu Sufyan, with his son (the future founder of the Umayyad dynasty) Mu'awiya, came to the tent of the

Prophet. There, at last, he confessed that there was no deity but the one God and that Muhammad was His messenger. Abu Sufyan asked only that he be allowed to fight the enemies of God as he had once fought the Muslims and that his son Mu'awiya become one of the Prophet's scribes.

The next day, the Muslims entered Mecca in a nearly bloodless conquest. The city's Muslims, who were by that time many, rejoiced. The Prophet had marked six Meccans for death. Among them was Ibn Khatal, who had become Muslim and then apostatized. Four were killed by Khalid's forces as they offered up armed resistance. As for the rest of the Quraysh, Muhammad granted amnesty to anyone who clung to the Kaba or entered the house of Abu Sufyan.

As the Muslims took control of the ancient city, Muhammad marched up to the Kaba, the House of God built by Abraham, to destroy the graven images condemned by God. Taking his staff, he smashed the idols of the Arabs. Muhammad then sat to instruct the Meccans about his religion, especially the Meccan women, who might be ignorant of many tenets of Islam. The keys to the Kaba were given back to the Quraysh family that had traditionally held them and that holds them until today.

The march of Islam, however, did not end with the conquest of Mecca. The Quraysh allies of the Hawazin and Thaqif tribes still maintained open hostilities with the Muslims and hoped to recover Mecca. Muhammad led his army, now swollen to 12,000 men, from Mecca to meet his opponents along the road at Hunayn, a day's march south of the city. Interestingly, to help fund the expedition, the Prophet had accepted a gift of money from a Meccan who had still not accepted Islam.

In the valley of Hunayn, the allied forces took the Muslim army by surprise, and it was only through the bravery of the Muslim warriors, the leadership of Khalid, and angelic aid sent from God that the Prophet and his army were able to accomplish a complete rout of the enemy. Amid the fury and confusion, one of those who stood firmly by Muhammad was Abu Sufyan. The Muslim victory was complete, and over 24,000 camels were taken as spoils of war in the course of the fighting.

Many of the fleeing Hawazin and also some inveterate opponents of Islam from the Quraysh sought refuge in the city of Taif, the home of the tribe of Thaqif. Muhammad thus marched on the city to lay siege. Under Khalid's able direction, the assault proceeded successfully. Muhammad ordered, however, that the Muslims kill no women, children, or slaves unless they took up arms against the Muslims. When the town eventually submitted much later, the Muslims took 6,000 women and children prisoner. Thaqif surrendered and embraced Islam as a group. Muhammad sent one of his bodyguards, Mughira bin Shu'ba, to destroy the idol Lat with an axe.

This was not a time only of victory, however. The Prophet faced his first unmitigated defeat and lost close family members as well. A few months earlier, the Prophet had sent a large expeditionary force north to meet some of the northern Arab tribes who had expressed hostility towards the Muslims. Led by Muhammad's adopted son Zayd and cousin Ja'far, the Muslim army met a vastly superior Byzantine force at the field of Muta south of the Dead Sea. In the course of the ensuing fighting, both Zayd and Ja'far fell as martyrs. Only Khalid's competent leadership was able to save the remaining Muslim soldiers from slaughter as the army retreated back to Medina.

Healing old wounds and expansion

When Taif surrendered, the last obdurate opponents of Islam were left with no refuge. After the conquest of Mecca and Taif, Muhammad pursued a course of action that was both merciful and practical with those who had formerly been enemies of Islam.

It was made known that anyone who became Muslim and sought the Prophet's reprieve would not be turned away. Among those who came before Muhammad to announce their conversion to Islam after Taif fell was Wahshi, the slave whom Hind had hired to kill Hamza at the Battle of Uhud. Muhammad asked Wahshi how Hamza had died and then sent him away in peace. 'One man's Islam is dearer to me than the slaying of a thousand unbelievers', concluded Muhammad. Even Hind, Abu Sufyan's wife, who had eaten Hamza's liver, was accepted as a Muslim by the Prophet.

God referred to the defeated Quraysh, Thaqif, and the Hawazin as 'those whose hearts are to be reconciled' in the Quran (9:60) and ordered Muhammad to present these defeated Meccans with the bulk of the spoils of war from the Battle of Hunayn.

Placating the Quraysh, however, came at the expense of others. The Helpers now found themselves out of favour. It was their share of the Hunayn spoils that were given to the newly converted Meccans – people who had until a few weeks before been desperate opponents of Muhammad! Leaders of the Helpers complained bitterly to the Prophet, who consoled them by saying that their spoils from the conflict was that he, the Messenger of God, now was theirs and belonged to their city.

Perhaps the most dramatic plea for peace with Muhammad came from the famous Arab poet Ka'b bin Zuhayr, who had written satirical verses about the Prophet. Muhammad had ordered his assassination, and now that the Muslim star was reaching its apogee, Ka'b had little choice but to appeal to Muhammad's mercy. He did so through a poem praising Muhammad and his Quraysh descent in the beauteous language and desert imagery that so moved the Arabs. So touched was the Prophet when he heard Ka'b recite the composition that he not only forgave him, he cast upon Ka'b's shoulders his own Yemeni cloak, or *burda*, by which name the poem was to be known.

In the summer of 630, Muhammad's informants among the northern Arab tribes reported that Byzantine forces were again grouping in the north of the Arabian Peninsula. Eager to confront those who had killed his kin the year before at the Battle of Muta, Muhammad mustered his forces once more. But the Muslim soldiers had by now returned to Medina, and the summer heat and exhaustion led many to grumble bitterly at these orders. Many Muslims simply refused to take part in the campaign, proffering various excuses such as the impending date harvest. To help remedy this shortage of assistance, Abu Bakr, Umar, and Uthman gave most of their personal wealth to the Prophet to fund the campaign.

Muhammad led his troops to the north, leaving Ali in charge of Medina. When he arrived at the desert settlement of Tabuk, Muhammad ordered his troops to make camp. Concerned over the shortage of water, the Prophet struck a rock with his staff and water gushed forth from it. After waiting for ten days, however, and with no sign of the Byzantine army, the Prophet ordered the Muslims to break camp.

The campaign, however, was not fruitless. The Prophet accepted the submission of the Christian Arab tribes living in the town of Ayla on the Gulf of Aqaba. These Christians agreed to pay the *jizya* tax to Medina in return for protection and in order to continue practising their own religion.

The Master of Arabia

With Mecca now in Muslim hands, Islam was now the most powerful force in Arabia and Muhammad the most powerful man. For the Arab tribes who had not yet sided with the lord of Medina, the choice became clear. Delegates from the great tribes of Arabia came to Muhammad to pledge their allegiance to the Messenger of God: the great Najd tribes of Tamim and Hanifa, the Yemeni tribes of Tayy and Hamdan. They embraced Islam and agreed to pay the charitable tithe to Medina.

The year spanning 630–1 thus became known as the 'Year of the Delegations'. The Quran reminded Muhammad to remain humble even in these great days of triumph: 'When God's succour and victory come, and you see the people entering God's religion in waves, extol the praise of your Lord, indeed He is most accepting of repentance' (Quran 110).

The tension that arose around the Tabuk campaign brought the problem of hypocrisy into unprecedented relief. With power came wealth and influence, and many new converts to Islam were clearly not true believers or committed to Muhammad's mission. The Prophet became increasingly impatient with the known hypocrites in Medina. He even divulged, in secret, their names to his Companion Hudhayfa bin al-Yaman, who would serve as the keeper of apocalyptic secrets among the Companions. During one Friday sermon, Muhammad angrily expelled 36 hypocrites from the mosque. Grieving at his isolation, the arch-hypocrite 'Abdallah bin Ubayy died. Although Umar cautioned him not to pray for the soul of this despicable character, Muhammad's mercy overcame him and he prayed to God to forgive 'Abdallah. The Quran, however, ruled in favour of Umar and ordered the Prophet never again to pray for the forgiveness of deceased hypocrites.

Although all the believers were equal in standing before God's law, the Muslim community around Muhammad now had noticeable degrees of commitment and loyalty. At the heart of the Muslim community, the *umma*, was the tightly knit body of Emigrants such as Abu Bakr, Umar, Ali, and Aisha, many of whom were intermarried with one another's families. Also in this core group were the elite Helpers such as Sa'd bin 'Ubada and 'Abdallah bin Salam. The next layer removed were those Muslims who had risked their lives at the early Battle of Badr, known as the 'People of Badr', and praised in the Quran as being forgiven whatever sins they might commit.

Beyond these loyal followers, there were new converts to Islam from the Quraysh, the tribes that allied with Medina early on, and now the hordes of distant Bedouin tribes who had entered Islam in a wave of victorious momentum but who had little idea of the religion in whose name they fought. To these fair-weather converts, the Quran tells the Prophet to say, 'You believe not, but rather say "We submit", for faith has not yet entered into your hearts. Yet, if you obey God and His messenger, He will not withhold from you any reward for your deeds. Indeed God is Forgiving, Merciful' (Quran 49:14).

After the conquest of Mecca, no more polytheists would be allowed to attend the great annual pilgrimage in the city. In the year nine of the *Hijra*, Muhammad remained in Medina and sent Abu Bakr to lead the Muslims in their *Hajj* to the Kaba. The Quran announced that the tribes which had not converted to Islam or entered into a treaty with Muhammad would have four months of respite. Then the Muslims would 'fight the polytheists wherever they found them' unless they converted to Islam or agreed to pay the *jizya* tax and submit to the rule of the Muslim state (Quran 9:5–7).

The last days of the Messenger of God

It is not clear how old Muhammad was the year he died, probably 63, but his hair had not yet been flecked by grey, and he remained virile and full of spirit. After the Year of Delegations, however, the Prophet became increasingly distant in some ways. He would go frequently to the cemetery outside of Medina and pray for the dead interred there.

The faith that Muhammad had once not dared preach openly in the streets of his own town of Mecca was now espoused from

Yemen to the River Jordan. Across Arabia, the Messenger of God was honoured. Now, for the first time since Abraham's pure monotheism had been corrupted by pagan practices, the sacred precinct of Mecca was free of idols. In March of 632, Muhammad at last led an unencumbered *Hajj* to the House of God built for the worship of the one God alone.

Circumambulating the Kaba in the white pilgrim's garb, Muhammad was thronged by crowds and had to mount a camel to rise above the swarm. On the plain of Arafat outside of Mecca, where as part of their pilgrimage rituals Muslims rest and pray one day from noon to sunset, the Prophet addressed his many thousands of followers (as many as 40,000) for what would be his last major speech. The Prophet told his followers to heed his words on that day and in that place, for it might well be that they would never see him again. That day, he told the Muslims, God had revealed the capstone verse of the Quran: 'Today I have perfected for you your religion, and completed My blessing upon you, and have willed Submission (Islam) for you as your religion' (Quran 5:3).

In what became known as his 'Farewell Sermon', Muhammad reminded the Muslims of the five pillars of Islam: belief in the one God and His Messenger, prayer, charity, fasting, and the pilgrimage to Mecca. He annulled all usurious loans carried over from the time before Islam and enjoined Muslim men to treat their women with kindness: 'You have rights over your wives, and your wives have rights over you.' 'All the Muslims are brothers', he preached. 'The Arab is not superior to the non-Arab, nor the non-Arab to the Arab.' All races and colours are equal, 'except in their fear of God'.

Returning to Medina after the *Hajj*, Muhammad stopped his caravan at a small pool called Ghadir Khumm. There, before all his retinue, he took Ali's hand and announced, 'Whoever's master I am, Ali is his master.' Not long after his return to Medina,

Muhammad ordered a military expedition to be prepared against
the Byzantines.

Soon thereafter, the Prophet fell ill, suffering from a severe
headache. One day, as he was conducting his affairs, Muhammad
could not stand. His cousin Fadl, the son of his uncle Abbas,
and Ali carried the ailing Messenger of God to Aisha's quarters
in the mosque.

Muhammad was not well enough to lead prayers in the mosque,
so he instructed his oldest friend Abu Bakr to take his place.
Fatigued by people's concern over him, he muttered to his wives
that all the doors of the city's houses be closed except the door of
Abu Bakr. Others say that he said only Ali's door. A few days
later, Muhammad felt well enough to enter the courtyard of the
mosque during prayers. Sensing him approaching from behind,
Abu Bakr instinctively moved backwards to make room for the
Prophet to take over. But Muhammad pressed his hand against
his friend's back and pushed him gently back into the leader's
position. After prayers, Muhammad climbed the pulpit for one
final sermon. He warned the Muslims not to fall into internecine
strife or glorify him unduly as the Christians had done to Jesus.
Then the Prophet returned to Aisha's house.

There was tremendous worry amongst the Muslims in Medina,
especially among Muhammad's close retinue of advisors. What
would happen if the unthinkable occurred and their Prophet was
taken from them? Who would lead? Abbas went with Ali to Aisha's
house to seek out the Prophet's last will and testament. Abbas knew
this was the end – 'I know what death looks like in the faces of the
descendants of 'Abd al-Muttalib.' He urged Ali to enter and ask the
Prophet who should succeed him. But Ali could only reply, 'If he
denies us authority today, none after him will ever grant it to us.'

In his final illness, however, Muhammad made no recorded will
as to who should succeed him. Some Companions would later

recall that Muhammad had ordered three things done in this final days: he divided up his remaining lands from the Khaybar spoils and assigned them to certain followers, he ordered that his campaign against the Byzantines continue as planned, and he ordered that only one religion, Islam, be allowed in the peninsula of the Arabs. In another report on the Prophet's last orders, Abbas recalls commands to maintain alliances and to free Arabia of other religions but could not remember the third order.

Muhammad's family gathered around him in Aisha's house as he lay ill. He called his daughter Fatima to him and whispered in her ear. She began to weep, but he whispered again, and she smiled. Later, she would recount that he had first told her that God had given him the choice of remaining amongst the living or 'journeying to the Highest Companion'. He had chosen death. But Fatima had found joy when her father told her that she would be the first of his family to join him in heaven. Indeed, she would die six months after him.

As Muhammad's illness intensified, he wrapped his head in blankets to help ease the pain. He rested his head on Aisha's lap as he sweated in agony from his headache. Occasionally, he would call for the *miswak*, the fibrous twig used to clean one's teeth. Aisha later recalled that the last thing Muhammad did was to call for a pot to relieve himself. Soon afterwards, she felt his spirit leave him. It was 8 June 632.

In the courtyard of the mosque just outside Aisha's room, the Muslims of Medina sat gathered in trepidation at the imminent loss of their leader and focal point of their lives. When rumours began circulating that Muhammad had died, Umar raised his voice above the crowd and threatened to slay on the spot anyone who said the Messenger had passed away. Umar believed that Muhammad had journeyed to heaven as Moses had, and just like Moses he would return. But Abu Bakr rose beside his friend and, in that moment, reminded the Muslims of their faith. 'Whoever worshipped Muhammad, know that he is dead. But whoever worships God, know that He is forever living and never dies.'

Despite this reminder, panic struck the Muslims as different cliques and families returned to their homes to discuss what to do. In Aisha's room, Ali began preparations for washing Muhammad's body for burial. Abu Bakr had rightly noted that 'God never took a prophet except that he should be buried in the place where he died.'

In the meantime, the leading members of the Helpers had gathered to debate the future of their city apart from the Emigrants. Hearing about this, Umar rushed with Abu Bakr and other leading Emigrants to try to mend an impending split in the *umma*. If there were to be any unity amongst the Muslims, the Helpers argued, there should be two leaders to succeed Muhammad: one from the Helpers and one from the Emigrants. But Umar and Abu Bakr insisted that, as the *umma* was one, so too its leader should be one. Umar nominated Abu Bakr and the Helpers accepted. He was the only man they would follow, since it was he whom the Prophet had taken as his companion during the *Hijra*, 'one of the two who were in the cave' (Quran 9:40).

So at this crucial hour, while Ali washed the Prophet's body with his womenfolk, the Muslim community embraced its first caliph (Arabic *khalifa*), or Successor to the Messenger of God. Muhammad was buried three days later beneath the dirt floor of Aisha's house. Muhammad was gone now, and only his Companions could preserve the memory and teachings of the man they had come to venerate so dearly.

Chapter 2
Shaping Muhammad in history

The narrative in Chapter 1 is a digest of the most famous Muslim biography of Muhammad, the *Sira* (biography) written by the Arab historian Ibn Ishaq (d. 767) (pronounced Is-haq). Unlike what you have just read in this book, however, the original *Sira* was not a narrative like the ones we are accustomed to reading, nor was Ibn Ishaq an author in the sense that I am.

The *Sira*, and other books like it, were the products of early Muslim historians whose work revolved around individual reports known as *akhbar* (plural of *khabar*, or 'report'). Like a journalist, a Muslim historian such as Ibn Ishaq would collect numerous reports about an event from different sources: the testimony of eyewitnesses to an event, people who had met eyewitnesses, interviews with other scholars of history, and earlier written collections of *akhbar*. The historian would then select which reports he wanted to include in constructing his story. The book he eventually produced would consist of thousands of reports in roughly chronological order, each one introduced by the authority from whom he had received the report and often including the chain of people who had transmitted it from the eyewitness.

Muslim historians like Ibn Ishaq would select which reports were most reliable based on their opinion of their sources' reliability. They would also try to assure that a source had received his reports

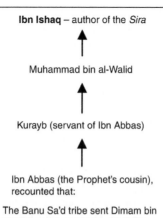

Ibn Ishaq – author of the *Sira*

↑

Muhammad bin al-Walid

↑

Kurayb (servant of Ibn Abbas)

↑

Ibn Abbas (the Prophet's cousin), recounted that:

The Banu Sa'd tribe sent Dimam bin Tha'laba as an ambassador to the Messenger of God…He asked the Messenger, 'I ask you in the name of your god, the god of those before you and the god of those yet to come, truly did God send you as a prophet?'

4. An example of a *khabar* that Ibn Ishaq included in his *Sira*

from an eyewitness via an unbroken chain of transmitters. When reports conflicted or contradicted one another, Ibn Ishaq had to choose which one was more reliable or include both versions (for example, we saw the conflicting reports about Muhammad's last will and testament). There were significant differences amongst early Muslim historians on important events in the Prophet's life. Was he 63 or 65 when he died? Musa bin 'Uqba (d. 758), an early scholar of the Prophet's campaigns, held that the night journey to heaven occurred one year before the *Hijra*, but another early scholar, al-Zuhri (d. 742), said seven years before.

Of course, Ibn Ishaq's choices about which reports were reliable or realistic and which ones merited inclusion were governed by his own religious views and the forces influencing him. The Muslim historian was thus much more an editor than an author. He expressed his opinions about what had happened in the past not through his prose and written analyses, but through his choices about including and excluding reports.

The Arabs of the Prophet's time had no tradition of written history. Memories of their tribal battles were preserved in poetry and tales that were passed on orally. Arabs also paid great attention to genealogy. In addition, Jewish, Christian, and Zoroastrian lore circulated amongst the Arabs like folk tales.

The earliest Islamic historical writing built on these interests. Muslim scholars compiled reports about the campaigns, or *maghazi*, of the Prophet and his Companions. Books of genealogy, *ansab*, were also composed. Muslims with Jewish or Zoroastrian backgrounds devoted special attention to stories of earlier prophets, known as *qasas*. In addition, Muslim scholars attempted to trace when and where various Quranic verses had been revealed in order to understand their meaning. Such works on Quranic commentary were known as *tafsir*.

Ibn Ishaq drew on all this material in composing his *Sira*. With the exception of a few scraps of papyrus and parchment, however, no original copy of the *Sira* has survived until today. Furthermore, we do not even have a complete copy made of Ibn Ishaq's original book. Instead, what we have is an edition of the *Sira* produced decades later by an Egyptian scholar named Ibn Hisham (d. 833). Ibn Hisham found some of the material that Ibn Ishaq included objectionable, such as the story of the Prophet contemplating suicide after his first revelation and the Satanic Verses (see below). He removed such reports as well as the entire first section of the work, which covered the history of the world (from a very Abrahamic point of view) from Adam and Eve until Muhammad's birth. Ibn Hisham also added his own selection of stories about Muhammad. Nevertheless, modern historians have tried to reconstruct Ibn Ishaq's original work by locating his reports in other Muslim historical works of the 9th and 10th centuries.

Ibn Hisham's edition of the *Sira* became the most widely read and influential biography of the Prophet. Other Muslim scholars also wrote *sira*s, both before and after that of Ibn Ishaq/Ibn Hisham. The early Muslim historians al-Zuhri (d. 742), Wahb bin Munabbih (d. 732), and Abu Ma'shar (d. 780) compiled *sira*s that Ibn Ishaq sometimes consulted in his work. The biography of Muhammad written by the 14th-century Syrian scholar Ibn Kathir (d. 1373) gained a great deal of popularity, but no work has been as definitive as Ibn Hisham's edition of the *Sira*. It became the reference for the basic chronology for the Prophet's life (for example, when the night journey occurred). Furthermore, this *Sira* accords with and represents orthodox Sunni Islam, but it also has tremendous popular appeal. One 13th-century scholar even rendered Ibn Hisham's book in poetry form.

When non-Muslims read the *Sira* today, they are often struck by its many foreign elements (marrying a girl believed to have been ten years old, for example, and *jinn*), but also by the numerous parallels to narratives familiar to Christian audiences (such as multiplying food and healing the sick). By examining the world into which Muhammad was born and how his biography was written, we can better understand how the story of Muhammad developed and determine its historical reliability.

The pre-Islamic Near Eastern and Arabian context

Muhammad's career was a turning point in world history, but he was very much a child of his time. The story of his life and mission were outgrowths of Arabia and the greater Near Eastern world of the 6th and 7th centuries CE. Many elements that might strike us as foreign or bizarre in the *Sira* fit together in their own logic when viewed in this context.

The world of Muhammad was the world of late antiquity, a period of intense change in the Near East between roughly 250 CE and the rise of Islam. In the eastern Mediterranean, the shared culture of the Roman Empire transformed from the inclusive paganism of Greco-Roman religion to the intensely Christian world of Byzantium (the eastern half of the Roman Empire which survived the fall of Rome). The many gods and cults of Roman polytheism were replaced by Christian saints and holy men.

The religious world of people living in Syria, the Holy Land, and Iraq on the eve of Muhammad's birth was permeated by the supernatural. Men and women believed they lived side by side with an unseen world of evil demons and goodly spirits who interacted with humans. Malevolent demons possessed people's bodies, causing illness or insanity, and Christian holy men would be called to drive them out and heal the sick. Other demons and devils wrought mischief amongst men, causing people to lose things or revealing to them dark and dangerous secrets. We even find stories of demons copulating with humans. These demons and spirits are portrayed in writings as ghoulishly hybrid animals, such as creatures with the head of a cat, a cleft tongue, and walking on two legs.

Other spirits from this parallel world were helpful and beneficent. A type of spirit known as a 'companion' (Arabic, *qarin*) was born at the same time as a person to protect and guide them. Like a guardian angel, this was the late antique version of the 'genius', or tutorial spirit, of the classical Roman emperors to whom all Romans had to offer prayers. Mani (d. 276 CE), a Persian from Iraq who claimed to be both the restorer of Zoroastrianism and the last Apostle of Christ, began his mission when his companion spirit appeared to him as he looked at his reflection in the water. We find these good and bad spirits mentioned as *ginnaye* in Aramaic (the Semitic language of the Fertile Crescent and Holy Land before Arabic) rock inscriptions near the great 3rd-century Syrian trading city of Palmyra.

These *ginnaye* are part of the same broad phenomenon as the Arabic *jinn* that Muhammad encountered one night in the desert. The Quran specifically tells us that these creatures are the counterparts of men: 'I did not create the *jinn* and mankind except to worship Me' (Quran 51:56). Muslim lore includes many stories analogous to earlier Near Eastern tales about the supernatural, such as *jinn* marrying human women. In one story from Arabia at the time of the Prophet, a *jinn* who had been carrying on an affair with an Arab woman regretfully cuts off their relationship when the Quran forbids fornication. The household shrines of Arabs in towns like Yathrib resembled the Roman *lars* and *penates*, or the guardian spirits of Roman homes.

Humans could access and manipulate this supernatural world so real to the population of the late antique Near East. It was accepted as entirely possible and even normal for certain men and women to have powers of magic or preternatural foresight. If such people were perceived as good and rightly guided, they were heralded as prophets, oracles, or saints. When an individual claiming such contact with the divine was rejected by his community, it was not because the claim itself was ludicrous. It was because that person was seen as manifesting some link with the supernatural in an evil or destructive manner. In other words, it was a question of good magic or bad, not whether magic existed. The most common accusation against such 'bad magic' was that of sorcery. It was on charges of sorcery that many Christian martyrs in the eastern Mediterranean were executed during the first three centuries CE.

It is thus no surprise that the Quraysh did not dismiss Muhammad for merely claiming that God or prophecy existed – everyone agreed they did (only once does the Quran address the issue of pure and simple atheism; Quran 45:24). Rather, the Quraysh accused Muhammad of being a sorcerer (*sahir*) who destroyed communities by splitting those he enchanted away from their families. The Quraysh's argument that the Quran was merely 'the words of a soothsayer' (Quran 69:42) resonated with people sceptical of Muhammad because prognosticating soothsayers called *kahins* spouting rhymed prose were a routine part of Arab religious life. Perhaps the 'foreign teacher' that the Quraysh accused Muhammad of learning the Quran from was an evil companion spirit or a sorcerer bent on undermining their way of life.

The figure of the holy man or saint was another constant feature of the late antique world. Christian saints were possessed of astounding powers through their proximity to God. For example, the 4th-century Syrian saint Jacob of Nisibis was said to be able to explode boulders with mere words. The famous founder of monasticism, St Anthony of Egypt (d. 356), retreated into the desert for twenty years to encounter and defeat demons. He returned to society able heal the sick and even resurrect the dead. St Simeon (d. 459), who lived for forty years as an ascetic atop a pillar in the Syrian desert, was immune to mortal needs like hunger and thirst. Other saints could read minds or become invisible. Figures like St Simeon were so revered by Christians in the cities around them that urbanites and even rulers came to them for prayers and to resolve disputes.

One of the most immediate connections between the Christian saint and the laity was the saint's body, alive or dead. Physical remains of his clothing, hair, blood, or even his bones became vehicles of holiness and blessing. In 415 CE, the remains of St Steven were supposedly discovered in a village north of Jerusalem. The population flocked to his coffin, which emitted perfume of heavenly sweetness, and the sick were healed. Those devout Christians who were wealthy enough would travel to distant cities to touch or be in the presence of a saint's relics.

Muhammad's career mirrored that of a Near Eastern holy man in many ways. Abandoning Mecca for the desert, meditating in a cave, and his visions of Gabriel would have been seen as standard preludes to a prophetic mission. The stories of his miracles in the *Sira*, such as his healing the eye of a man wounded in battle, are impossible to miss. Like St Simeon, the Prophet's status as a holy man granted him great temporal power and the ability to mediate social feuds; the people of Yathrib sought him out to resolve their internal disputes. Muhammad fasted so much that he had to warn his followers not to imitate him too closely. 'I am not like you', he supposedly said, 'Indeed I am given food and drink [by God].' Like St Simeon, he too seemed immune to hunger and thirst.

The Companions' obsession with the Prophet's person, his hair, water that he had spat out, and even his blood, reflects late antique veneration of the saint's body (tasting the Prophet's blood may also have been an expression of Arabian customs of creating kinship or alliances by two parties intermingling and licking each other's blood). Like the bones and blood of a saint, emissions and remnants of the Prophet's body were vehicles of blessings and contact with God.

Of course, we must note important differences between Muhammad and Christian holy men. Muhammad was a religious figure engaged in every aspect of social life. He was no monk, enjoying an active married life. More importantly, he did not remain outside of society. His desert retreat was brief, and as a prophet his role was as a leader within society and inside the city.

The role of the Jewish rabbinical master provided another important pattern for Muhammad's career. As inheritors of the teachings of Moses and the Hebrew prophets, the rabbis of late antiquity were viewed as living examples of how the Torah should be lived in daily life. Their students copied how they bathed and ate, and were even known to hide under their master's bed to observe how he made love to his wife. Once, one of Rabbi Akiva's (d. 135 CE) students stole into the bathroom behind his teacher to learn which directions one should face and how to clean oneself.

Muhammad's Companions too looked to the minutest details of his conduct for insights into the behaviour and lifestyle that most pleased God. Their imitation of his dress and repetition of the prayers he said when eating or drinking were passed on and became enshrined in Islamic law. We find a direct analogy to Akiva's student in the Companions' boast that their Prophet had taught them everything, 'even how to defecate'.

Some aspects of Muhammad's life reflect common elements of the Near Eastern heritage. The notion of an ascent to heaven led by an angelic escort appears in many Near Eastern religious and literary works. In Virgil's (d. 19 BCE) epic the *Aenead*, the hero Aeneas is shown the underworld by an oracular guide. One of the Jewish texts found among the Dead Sea Scrolls references a lost Jewish book called *The Assumption of Moses*, which describes Moses' journey up through the heavens and back.

Ezra, who led the Jewish tribes after their return from the Babylonian exile in the 5th century BCE, is also described as having ascended to heaven. Like the Prophet having his heart cleansed in a bowl of wisdom in heaven, Ezra is given a cup of liquid the colour of fire. This drink gives him the inspiration needed to reconstitute the Torah.

In the *Apocalypse of Paul*, an apocryphal Christian text dating from around 300 CE, the apostle Paul is portrayed recounting his mystical visit to the heavens and return to earth. Ascending through ten levels of heaven, Paul sees 3,000 angels singing hymns of praise and meets the earlier prophets. Muhammad's night journey to Jerusalem, tour of the heavens, vision of angels, and so on thus echoed a common theme of prophecy in the Near East.

The feature of the late antique religious world that is the most instructive in understanding Muhammad's career is the conflict between an inclusive polytheism and an exclusive monotheism. In the expansive Roman Empire, it seemed obvious to Roman officials and their pagan subjects that different gods ruled or tended to different peoples. The Empire thus welcomed the varied religious beliefs and practices of its diverse peoples, provided they agreed to offer incense sacrifices to the guardian spirit of the Roman emperor. It was essential to respect and sacrifice to the imperial gods in order to maintain what the Romans called 'Peace of the Gods' (*pax deorum*) and ensure the continued prosperity of the Empire's population.

When a new religion emerged that insisted that only one god existed and refused to sacrifice at the altars of any other deities, the Roman officials were befuddled. Did these Christians not understand that by refusing to sacrifice to the emperor's guardian spirit they were endangering the Empire and its peoples by angering the gods? As the Emperor Trajan wrote to a Roman governor in 112 CE, these Christians were welcome to worship their god as long as they accepted that at least the imperial deities were worthy of honour as well.

The reaction of the Quraysh to Muhammad's radical monotheism echoed that of the Roman officials. It was not mere stubbornness or bigotry that motivated the Quraysh in their negotiations with Muhammad. The great God Allah was of course welcome at the Kaba along with the demigods who interceded with Him. But the Quraysh feared angering heaven, and rejecting all the other gods was to risk bringing supernatural ire down upon Mecca and ruining its prosperity.

Focusing more narrowly on the Arabian Peninsula of Muhammad's time, we find a context that further explains the man and his mission. The Arabian religious worldview placed great emphasis on sacred places and sacred times. Four of the pre-Islamic Arab months, which Islam adopted, were 'sacred' times during which fighting was prohibited. The notion of a *haram*, or sacred precinct, was widespread in Yemen and the Hejaz. In Yemen, these precincts were centres of worship for local gods and were often located at the intersection of valleys. With fighting prohibited in these *haram*s and religious pilgrimages guaranteed, markets would soon follow. Clans that could gain control of *haram*s would thus acquire a sacred prestige and the right to collect taxes there.

Located at the intersection of valleys on the northern fringe of the Yemeni mountains, Mecca was one of many *haram*s. The Quraysh was its custodian clan. When Muhammad established the Muslim community at Medina, he declared that city a *haram* as well. This was perhaps essential to succeed in his conflict with Mecca and prove his status as a prophet. As Muhammad is reported to have explained, 'Every prophet has a *haram*, and mine is Medina.'

Other inscrutable features of the *Sira* also make more sense when illuminated by the social context of pre-Islamic Arabia. The single most dominant reality of life there was the tribal system. With no government, laws, rights, or even a shared religion, pre-Islamic Arabs had only their tribes and the loyalty of this extended family to rely on for protection. Although pre-Islamic Arabic poetry sung of constant violent feuding, in the harsh climes of the desert, people could only survive by relying on their community and neighbours.

It is no surprise, then, that while the Muslims in Medina might battle other tribes who violated treaties or expel the Jewish tribes living on the outskirts of Medina, within the heart of Medina Muhammad refused to violently persecute even open opponents like the hypocrite 'Abdallah bin Ubayy.

Although Islam was based on the equality of all believers before God, the tribal system of Arabia preceded and sometimes superseded this principle. Like a preacher or politician in a modern democracy, Muhammad had to work within the system to succeed in altering it. In Medina, the Quran would instruct Muslims not to take non-Muslims as friends or protectors in preference to the bonds of Islam. Yet in Mecca, Muhammad had survived by availing himself of what one might call the 'constitutional rights' of his non-Muslim tribal society. Abu Talib and later Mut'im bin 'Adi, both infidels who rejected Muhammad's teachings, committed their family network to protecting the Prophet regardless of the enmity of the rest of the Quraysh. This stemmed from the overwhelming emphasis on protecting kinsmen within Arab society, an element of that society that Muhammad embraced to his advantage.

When the Prophet and his religion triumphed in Arabia, the power of the tribal system once again reared its head. Once Mecca was reconquered, the non-Quraysh Helpers generally fell by the wayside. Most of their share of the Hunayn spoils was given to Muhammad's clan, the Quraysh, to placate them after their defeat. When the Muslims expanded into the greater Near East, we find that the caliphs and Muslim governors were all either members of the Quraysh or clients from smaller tribes with no tribal interests of their own to pursue. The Helpers, despite their sacrifices in providing the cradle of Islam in Medina, never regained their former primacy (although the committee that compiled the Quran after Muhammad's death consisted of all Helpers).

Muhammad's marriages in context

More than any other feature of Muhammad's life, his many marriages have consistently struck and bewildered Western readers since the rise of Islam. The Prophet's polygamy and the Quranic ruling that Muslim men can marry up to four women at a time (the Prophet was allowed more because it was believed that he would never mistreat any of his wives) created early on in medieval Christendom an image of Muhammad as lustful.

Prior to Christianity, however, the Near East from Pharaonic Egypt to ancient Mesopotamia was a world in which polygamy was not foreign at all. For most men, it would have been too expensive, but for rulers or men of great import it was an expectable tool of politics and propagation. Perhaps the most famous exemplar for such 'harem politics' was King Solomon, whom the Bible says had 700 wives and 300 concubines (1 Kings 11). Among them was the daughter of the Pharaoh of Egypt, whom he had married to cement an alliance.

Indeed, when looked at through a political lens, Muhammad's marriages worked towards clear political goals. His marriage to Khadija, of course, had predated his prophethood, and she remained his only wife until she died. Let us look at whom the Prophet married after that and to whom he married his daughters. Muhammad married the daughters of Abu Bakr and Umar and married his own daughters to Uthman and Ali. These four men were the first four rulers of the Muslim state after the Prophet's death. Muhammad also married the daughter of Abu Sufyan as well as the sister of Abbas's wife, Maymuna (who was also the aunt of Khalid bin al-Walid). Abu Sufyan's son Mu'awiya founded the Umayyad caliphate after Ali's death in 660 CE, and Khalid was a leading general of the Muslim armies. The Prophet's marriages and those of his family thus helped create the network that provided the leadership of the Muslim community in the century after Muhammad's death.

The Prophet also entered into other politically potent marriages. He wed the daughter of the Jewish chief of Khaybar as well as numerous women from leading Arab tribes. The fact that we know nothing more than the tribal identities of two of these women further demonstrates that it was the political relationship that Muhammad was fostering that mattered.

There is nothing more controversial to the modern reader than Muhammad's marriage to Aisha, who is believed to have been between nine and ten years old when the marriage was consummated. (The most reliable historical sources on this marriage are the *Sahih* Hadith collections of al-Bukhari and Muslim (see Chapter 3)). Interestingly, no critic of Muhammad, from his fiercest opponents in the Quraysh to medieval Christian clerics, objected to his marriage to so young a wife until the modern period. This is noteworthy, since there has certainly never been a shortage of detractors seeking chinks in the armour of Muhammad's character to exploit.

It was his marriage to Zaynab, his adopted son's former wife, which attracted criticism even during Muhammad's own lifetime. The fact that Zayd is one of only two contemporaries of Muhammad ever mentioned in the Quran (the other is Abu Lahab), as well as the book's sizeable passage on the Zaynab episode, testifies to the controversy surrounding Muhammad's marriage to her. One of the earliest Christian polemicists against Islam, John of Damascus (d. 749), accused Muhammad of 'tailoring' the Quranic laws on marriage and adoption to legitimize his 'desire' for Zaynab. This accusation has been repeated endlessly throughout Christian writings on Islam. The 13th-century English historian Matthew Paris, for example, wrote in his great chronicle that Muhammad had pronounced polygamy permissible to cover up an affair with a servant's (presumably Zayd's) wife.

The reason that no pre-modern critics paid attention to the Prophet's marriage to a ten-year-old was because marrying girls considered underage today was commonplace in the pre-modern world. Under Roman law, the earliest permitted age for marriage was twelve. In the heyday of the Roman Empire (2nd century CE), by fourteen a girl was considered an adult whose primary purpose was marriage. In many pre-modern law codes, such as Hebrew biblical law and Salic Frankish law, marriage age was not a question at all. It was assumed that when a girl reached puberty and was able to bear children, she was ready for marriage.

As a result, we find that average marriage ages in the pre-modern world were remarkably young. Surviving evidence from several centuries of imperial Roman history suggests that as many as 8% of women married at ten or eleven. In Italy in the 1300s and 1400s, the average age for women was sixteen to seventeen. Even in an 1861 census in England, over 350 women married under the age of fifteen in just two counties that year. According to both Christian and Muslim teachings, the Virgin Mary was not the mature maternal figure seen in artwork about the Bible. She was at most in her mid-teens, having only just begun menstruating, and is reported to have been as young as ten years old.

Muhammad's decision to consummate his marriage to a ten-year-old would have been based on the same criteria as most pre-modern societies: Aisha's sexual maturity and readiness to bear a child. Consummation of the marriage would have occurred when she had menstruated and started puberty. As the great Muslim historian al-Tabari (d. 923) reported, 'At the time of her marriage contract Aisha was young and not capable of intercourse.' Three or four years later, however, she was able. Aisha herself would later remark that a girl can menstruate as young as nine and thus 'become a woman'.

Historical reliability and the formation of the *Sira*

The average Western audience would probably not find the Muslim biography of Muhammad entirely believable. It includes many miracles and assumes that God intervened in history by sending a prophet to establish Islam as the true religion. Such notions clash with the sentiments of many readers. Many today would reject the very notion of any one 'true' religion, since the dominant modern worldview does not associate truth with any particular faith tradition at all but rather with humanist values and an ongoing philosophical quest.

The modern Western discipline of writing history relies on an approach known as the 'Historical Critical Method' (HCM) to sort through stories about the past and to uncover what actually occurred. Although it is more of a toolbox of methods or mode of thinking than a fixed science, the HCM includes some basic approaches that govern how modern historians interrogate historical sources. From the point of view of historical reliability, the *Sira* presents two main problems for modern historians.

First, the *Sira* is a narrative that was not compiled during the lifetime of Muhammad himself. Ibn Ishaq only set it down on paper some 150 years after the Prophet's death. Furthermore, when the *Sira* was set down in book form, it was entirely the product of Muslims who by definition accepted Muhammad's religious claims.

These facts raise doubts in the minds of modern historians because they clash with the HCM's principal demand that historical sources be as close as possible chronologically to the events they describe, preferably from eyewitnesses. The HCM also demands that we take into consideration the biases of whomever serves as our source.

Western scholars inherited the first principle from Renaissance scholars who had advocated a return to the earliest available copies of a text to discover its original form. The basis for this is evident: the shorter the time that elapses between an event and the writing down of a report describing it, the less opportunity there is for error, forgetfulness, or intentional alteration to occur.

In the case of the *Sira*, we know that Ibn Ishaq did in fact rely on earlier sources and materials. With very few exceptions, however, our first record of these sources is Ibn Ishaq's work itself. We thus do not know if his sources really represented eyewitness reports or if they themselves had transformed or been doctored in the decades before Ibn Ishaq wrote.

Of course, even an eyewitness perceives an event from a certain point of view and interprets it according to his or her particular biases. Hence the requirement of modern historians that biases be taken into consideration. We cannot take our information about a war, for example, only from the victors; we also need the testimony of the defeated. By reading the words of both sides and by being sensitive to their biases and agendas, we can know when we can rely on a testimony or when not. The French historian and essayist Voltaire (d. 1778) wrote about the science of history, 'We can believe people in what they say about themselves if it is to their disadvantage.' This provides a central rule for modern historians: if a report contains something that makes its author or their side in a dispute look bad, it is probably true. Otherwise, why would they make it up?

The second problem with the *Sira* is that it is a sacred history that relies on faith claims and not modern historical methods. Major components of the *Sira* narrative, such as the assumption that Muhammad really was a prophet and that his community was chosen by God, ultimately hinge on the faith of the reader. A major principle of the HCM, however, is that nature and human societies function according to immutable laws, a principle handed down from the European Enlightenment. These immutable laws cannot be violated by miraculous occurrences, and it is natural and material forces that drive history, not the direct intercession of God. 'Let no god intervene', states the English historian James Froude (d. 1894), 'is a rule of history ...'. Modern historians are thus sceptical of narratives that paint too rosy a picture of a person or society, or portray them as dramatically different from the world we know. As Voltaire says, 'All ages resemble one another in respect of the criminal folly of mankind.'

The *Sira* and the historical Muhammad

For a modern historian, then, the story of a prophet, accompanied by miracles, destined to found God's true religion, and written down over a century later by his followers cannot be accepted at face value. If the *Sira* as we have it is not what *really* happened in Muhammad's life, then Western scholars have concluded that it must be a construction by the Muslims who came after him.

Those Muslims disagreed a great deal. In the immediate wake of Muhammad's death, the Muslim community was plunged into a crisis of leadership. Who would lead the community politically? More importantly, who would tell Muslims how to understand their religion now that their Prophet was gone? As the Muslims expanded into Iran and North Africa, they met strange new peoples and encountered unfamiliar customs and laws. How should Muslims live in this new world?

In the century after Muhammad's death, the Muslim community would pass through three civil wars to answer the questions of Muhammad's political succession. The party that developed into Shiite Islam believed that the Muslim community should be led by the family of the Prophet, in particular his descendants through Fatima and Ali, the Companion whom they believed was the best and most knowledgeable. Another group, known as the Kharijites, contended that it was only the most pious Muslim, regardless of his descent, who could legitimately lead. The movement that became Sunni Islam offered the most pragmatic answer: whichever leader the Muslim community as a whole accepted was legitimate. In effect, this legitimated the *status quo*; whoever could establish political control over the Muslims was the *de facto* legitimate ruler of the Muslim community.

In 656, Uthman, the third caliph to rule the Muslim community after Abu Bakr and Umar, was murdered in Medina by discontented rebels. Although the Prophet's son-in-law Ali believed that he himself should have succeeded the Prophet instead of Abu Bakr, he had contented himself with a background role in Muslim political life. With Uthman's death, however, Ali's supporters (known as the Shi'a, hence 'Shiites'), proclaimed him caliph. Mu'awiya, the son of Abu Sufyan and like Uthman a member of the Banu Umayya, protested the murder as well as Ali's assumption of power. Then the governor of Syria, Mu'awiya went to war with Ali in what became the First Civil War of Islam. Mu'awiya's victory in 660 marked the beginning of the Umayyad dynasty, which ruled until 750 CE.

In the mid-740s, a movement began in northeastern Iran that called for a return to rule by the Family of the Prophet and according to his Sunnah. The Umayyads, descendants of the former infidel Abu Sufyan, were seen by many Muslims as decadent and impious. The resistance movement took open form under a man named Abu al-Abbas al-Saffah, who was a descendant of the Prophet's uncle Abbas. In 750, this movement defeated the Umayyads and established what became the Abbasid dynasty. Ruling from their newly constructed imperial city of Baghdad, the Abbasid caliphs would remain the official leaders of the Sunni Muslim world until the Mongol sack of the city in 1258.

Perhaps more influential than these bloody political storms were the theological debates that confronted the Muslims as they came across the elaborate intellectual heritage of the Byzantine and Persian worlds. Where did Islam fit in relation to the ancient faiths of Judaism, Christianity, and Zoroastrianism? How should Muslims view Muhammad, and how did his person and mission compare to the founders of these earlier faith traditions? It is important to remember that, although the Islamic conquests of the Near East left Muslims in a position of temporal power, in terms of philosophical discussion, they were novices compared to rabbis and bishops.

The *Sira* was composed in the wake of, and in the midst of, these political conflicts, sectarian tensions, and interfaith debates. The persona of Muhammad, the founder of Islam and source of legitimacy amongst Muslims, was a central tool of propaganda. The parties involved in the civil wars and theological debates portrayed Muhammad in ways that suited their needs, and as a result the *Sira* bears the marks of these conflicts. In the language of art, then, we should not view the *Sira* as a uniform masterpiece created by one artist. It is more like a canvas that, while it conveys a coherent image, bears the streaks and sometimes irregular blotches of the many artists who had competed in painting it.

Certainly, much historical material about Muhammad was simply forged by partisans of sundry Muslim political or theological camps. But even those Muslims who believed they were authentically representing the person and life of the Prophet were affected by their own leanings. When we recall a departed loved one, the image we weave with the stories we remember or choose to tell cannot be an unprejudiced recreation of their life. It is always the result of who we understand that person to be or how we hope to portray them. So too the Muslims in the generations after Muhammad's death who remembered, transmitted, concocted, and selected stories about their Prophet were inevitably creating their own images of him.

In light of this reality, Western scholars have hotly debated the extent to which we can rely on the *Sira* as an historically reliable story of Muhammad's life. Who was Muhammad really? Can we accept the general outline of the *Sira* and merely reject those elements that do not accord with the Historical Critical Method, or is the whole narrative suspect?

Western historians from the Renaissance until today have generally accepted the overall Muslim narrative of Muhammad's life, rejecting only those elements and interpretations that clash with their respective worldviews. As with all scholarship, the way in which particular historians have addressed questions of reliability and the lens through which they have viewed Muhammad are coloured by their own beliefs and perspectives.

Medieval Western scholarship on Muhammad was deeply polemical, distorted by ignorance as much as by prejudice. An enormously popular 12th-century French epic, the *Song of Roland*, erroneously shows Muhammad as a demigod worshipped by Muslims: 'On the highest tower they raise [an image of] Mahomet, every one of the pagans prays to it and worships it.' A 14th-century English text tells that Muhammad had started off as a Christian who wanted to become pope. When he realized there was no place for him in Rome, however, he made his way to Syria, where he bewitched the Arabs into believing that he was a prophet.

In the case of historians writing from a Christian cultural perspective, such as Thomas Hobbes (d. 1679) in his classic *Leviathan*, this has meant rejecting the validity of Muhammad's claims to prophecy and interpreting him as an imposter.

For historians writing from a more secular perspective, Muhammad is seen as the sincere founder of a religion whose story accumulated the unfortunate build-up of human superstition and institutional meddling that encrusts all religions. This sympathetic but secular perspective imbues French Enlightenment works like Henri de Boulainvillier's (d. 1722) influential *Vie de Mahomed* (*Life of Muhammad*) and Voltaire's historical writings on the Prophet. Such European writers in the Enlightenment often crafted positive portrayals of Muhammad and the early Muslims not for their own sake but rather as foils to attack the Catholic Church or the Jews.

Historians of this early modern era, influenced by the growing centrality of nationalism in European life, often perceived an Arab national character to the Islamic conquests. As the peerless English historian of the Roman Empire Edward Gibbon (d. 1794) wrote, 'the Arabs ... had languished in poverty and contempt till Mahomet breathed into those savage bodies the soul of enthusiasm'.

Of course, residual European hostility towards Islam and contempt for religion in general strongly coloured the views of some modern historians even into the 20th century. The famous Swiss historian Jacob Burckhardt (d. 1897) called the dictator Julius Caesar 'the greatest of mortals', but condemned Muhammad as 'personally very fanatical' and rated the expansion of Islam as 'one of the greatest victories of fanaticism and triviality'.

Other historians like the Scottish Thomas Carlyle (d. 1881) viewed Muhammad as personifying a stage in the development of human civilization when prophets replaced kings and heroes. In Carlyle's eyes, Muhammad was sincere in his calling and belief in his own prophethood. His sincerity was in fact essential for the role of the prophetic leader to fully mature in human history.

Modern studies on Muhammad

Today, the most widely accepted scholarship on Muhammad has explained his mission chiefly from socio-economic and political angles. Like earlier historians, most scholars in recent years have accepted the broad outlines of the *Sira*. In its details and even in its structure, however, the *Sira* is now viewed as a story that developed over time as it was shaped by a Muslim community engaged in the construction of its own identity. As the Hungarian scholar Ignaz Goldziher (d. 1921) wrote, the *Sira* does not really tell us what Muhammad said or did, but rather it is 'a direct reflection of the aspirations of the Islamic community'. By reading the *Sira* as part of the development of Sunni Muslim orthodoxy, one can appreciate the layers that were added and covered over as Muslim identity grew.

The great modern scholar of Islam W. Montgomery Watt (d. 2006) epitomized a central tenet of modern historians studying Muhammad: 'A religion cannot come into being without sufficient motive.' According to Watt, the forces that drove Muhammad to bring Islam into being were economic and social. Watt describes Mecca in the half-century before Muhammad as experiencing a dramatic increase in wealth through trade. The city had become a centre of 'far-reaching and complicated mercantile operations'. As wealth increased among the Meccan elite, social change and economic tensions ensued. Livelihood moved from pastoral nomadism to trade, the central unit of society shifted from the tribe towards the individual, and the tribal moral code of the Arabs found itself under threat from increased wealth and greed.

As an orphan, Muhammad was excluded from the Meccan elite. His savvy marriage to the wealthy Khadija, however, had placed him in an intermediary position between the Meccan powerful and the increasingly disenfranchised poor. Muhammad's preaching, with its emphasis on social justice, charity, and individual moral responsibility before God, was a response to these tensions in Mecca and Arabia in general.

Viewed in light of the socio-economic and political motivations that underlay the founding of Islam, historians have detected a theme of realpolitik at the core of the *Sira*. The change of the direction of prayer from Jerusalem to Mecca seventeen months after the *Hijra* was not an act of divine fiat. When Muhammad had arrived in Medina, he had hoped that the Jewish tribes would join in his Abrahamic mission. When only a few converted to Islam, however, Muhammad shifted his attention from the Abrahamic city of Jerusalem back to the Arab centre of Mecca. Similarly, Muhammad's expulsions of the Jewish tribes from Medina were not the morally justified and divinely guided decisions of a prophet. They were the conscious strokes of a political actor gradually wrenching control of a city from powerful interest groups.

Modern historians read the details of the *Sira* from the outside in, peeling back the layers of narrative and propaganda that had built up as the Muslim community matured. The outermost layer is the world of Ibn Ishaq himself. Muhammad Ibn Ishaq spent the first part of his life in Medina. There he grew into an active and respected scholar of the Prophet's legacy. When he fell into a personal feud with the city's leading scholar, Malik bin Anas (d. 795), Ibn Ishaq moved to the newly erected city of Baghdad to seek his fortune at the Abbasid court. It was in Baghdad, in the shadow of the Abbasid caliphs, that he wrote his famous *Sira*. There are some reports that Ibn Ishaq actually wrote the *Sira* for the Abbasid dynasty and under its patronage. A Muslim scholar of the 13th century, al-Mundhiri, would later praise Ibn Ishaq for drawing the attention of the caliphal court to the study of Muhammad's biography.

It is therefore no surprise that the political context of the Abbasid caliphate left a noticeable impress on the *Sira*. Throughout the text, we find allusions to Abbasid legitimacy through the portrayal of their ancestor Abbas. Judging by the most obvious evidence, the Prophet's uncle Abbas was not a model Muslim. In fact, he and Muhammad's archenemy Abu Sufyan both only formally converted to Islam on the eve of the Muslim conquest of Mecca. Abbas never openly professed a belief in his nephew's faith during the Muslims' persecution in Mecca, nor did he make the sacrifice offered by so many of Muhammad's followers and leave his home in Mecca to immigrate to Medina. In fact, Abbas even participated in the Battle of Badr on the Meccan side!

Yet the *Sira* spins Abbas into an admirable figure. He was the caring advisor to the Prophet who accompanied his nephew during his negotiations with the Yathrib Muslims at 'Aqaba. The *Sira* excuses Abbas' late conversion by including reports that he had been a closet Muslim for years. Muhammad seemingly knew this, ordering his soldiers not to kill Abbas during the Battle of Badr and releasing him when he was captured. Ibn Hisham's edition of the *Sira* spells this out even more clearly, adding a comment that Abbas had already become Muslim in secret by the time of Badr.

The *Sira* often includes propaganda against the greatest opponents of the Abbasids during the first decades of their rule:

the Shiite 'Partisans of Ali'. Ibn Ishaq contrasts Abbas with Ali at seminal moments in the Prophet's life. For example, the work portrays Abbas as closer to the Prophet and more aware of his condition than Ali. It is Abbas who knows that the Prophet's final illness is mortal. His statement that 'I know what death looks like in the faces of the descendants of 'Abd al-Muttalib' emphasizes the closeness of his relation to Muhammad. He is his paternal uncle, a fellow son of 'Abd al-Muttalib, while as Muhammad's cousin Ali is one step further removed. The *Sira* has Ali implicitly undermine all later Shiite claims to political rule in Islam: 'If he denies us authority today', Ali says as the Prophet lies dying, 'none after him will ever grant it to us'. Since the *Sira* does not portray Muhammad bequeathing leadership to Ali upon his death, the reader should conclude that Ali's descendants would never lead.

The life of Muhammad was of utmost importance to the Sunni/Shiite conflict because the two sects divided on the question of whom the Prophet wanted to succeed him. Sunnis and Shiites therefore produced swathes of propaganda attempting to cast either Abu Bakr or Ali in the best possible light.

Ibn Ishaq adhered to what would become Sunni Islam, and the *Sira* is a distinctly Sunni vision of Muhammad's life. Nonetheless, so many Muslims living in the early Islamic period were Shiite or leaned towards the legitimacy of the Family of the Prophet that the *Sira* bears the marks of strong Shiite influence.

One major battlefield for Sunni/Shiite propaganda was the honour of being Muhammad's first male follower (Khadija was his first follower altogether). Ibn Ishaq states that 'Ali was the first male to believe in the Messenger of God', adding that Zayd was the second and Abu Bakr the third. From reconstructions of Ibn Ishaq's original *Sira*, however, it seems that he also included a report in which the ten-year-old Ali did not convert until after Abu Bakr because he said he needed to consult with his father Abu Talib.

These conflicting reports were probably the result of Ibn Ishaq trying to negotiate tensions between Sunni and Shiite reports and the sentiments of the two sects.

The question of Muhammad's final will and testament was even more sensitive. In the *Sira*, Ibn Ishaq includes a report in which only Ali accepts the Prophet's earliest overture of Islam to the Banu Hashim. Muhammad then says of him, 'This is my brother and my inheritor, heed him and obey him.' But this endorsement rings hollow as the Prophet's final days approach. It is Abu Bakr whom Muhammad commands to lead the communal prayers in his place. Ibn Ishaq includes another report that in his last speech Muhammad stated, 'If I could take anyone as a bosom friend, I would take Abu Bakr.' Neither of the two reports that the *Sira* includes about the Prophet's final orders makes any mention of succession or of Ali.

The *Sira* was not shaped only by internal Muslim debates. Muhammad personified Islam as a religion and the identity of the Muslim community. As a result, his biography had to portray a figure worthy of ruling over the pantheon of past Near Eastern prophets. The story of Muhammad had to impress Christians, Jews, and Zoroastrians.

These were not empty, abstract concerns. Muslim scholars in the 8th and 9th centuries faced open debates and the written polemics of Christian theologians. We must remember that, although Muslims were political rulers, they were a minority in the lands they conquered. The accusations of John of Damascus and Theodore Abu Qurrah, a 9th-century Syrian bishop, are good examples. Abu Qurrah wrote that the truth of Jesus' message was evident in his 'birth without the aid of seed, and by a mother unjoined to a man, and by a birth from a virgin'. John asserted that the coming of Jesus had been foretold since the time of Moses. No one, he claimed, had predicted Muhammad's mission.

Stories about Muhammad had to answer these objections. Establishing harbingers of Muhammad's coming was thus a major theme of the Quran and the *Sira*. In the *Sira*, the Prophet's pregnant mother is told by an angelic voice that she carries in her womb 'the lord of his people' and is commanded to name him 'The Most Praised'. This parallels the Gospel of Luke (1:30–3), where Gabriel announces the birth of Jesus to Mary. 'Do not be afraid, Mary', Gabriel assures her in the Bible, 'for you have found favour with God. And now, you will conceive in your womb and bear a son, and you will name him Jesus ... He will reign over the house of Jacob for ever ...'. Lights emanate from Amina's belly and illuminate the castles of Syria, a foreshadowing of the Muslim conquest of those Christian lands. Here we see echoes of the birth of another titan of the Near East: the historian Plutarch (d. c. 120 CE) reports that the night before her marriage, Alexander the Great's mother dreamt that her womb was struck by lightning. Like the nativity story of Jesus, stars descending mark the night of Muhammad's birth. A Jewish wise man announces the month of the Prophet's birth, crying from a hilltop 'Under this star shall be born The Most Praised (Ahmad)'.

Both the Quran and the *Sira* assert that Christian and Jewish scriptures predicted the coming of a prophet called 'The Most Praised', which in Arabic can be translated as Muhammad or Ahmad. In his *Sira*, Ibn Ishaq directly states that Muhammad was the Paraclete (commonly translated in English as 'Comforter' or 'Counsellor') whom Jesus foretells in the Gospel of John (14:16, 26). This association of Paraclete with the names Muhammad/Ahmad was based on a reading of the Greek word *parakletos* as *paraklutos*, meaning 'celebrated, praised'. The Muslims were not the first to make this claim – in the 3rd century, Mani (the founder of Manichaenism) had claimed to be the foretold Paraclete as well.

It was the challenge of miracles that proved most daunting for Muslims. Abu Qurrah argued that Jesus' power had been proven by healing the sick, raising the dead, and 'the satisfaction of many thousand from a few loaves and fish'. What had Muhammad done? A mysterious Christian writer in Baghdad in the 800s, 'Abd al-Masih al-Kindi, wrote that Jesus had miraculously healed a man's severed ear the night he was arrested at the Gethsemane. But when the Companion Talha lost a finger deflecting a sword blow from the Prophet at Uhud, al-Kindi claims, Muhammad was unable to heal his wounded Companion.

The *Sira* answered these challenges with a plethora of miracles matching those of earlier prophets. The Prophet multiplied food and water on many occasions (understandably, he did not turn water into wine!). He repaired the eye of one of his Companions during battle, and healed Ali's blindness before Khaybar. His visions of lights illuminating Syria, Yemen, and Iran presaged the imminent victories of Islam. A spider web was woven with preternatural speed over the cave in which he hid on the *Hijra*, and he split the moon in half on command.

Many of these miraculous stories seem to have come from the legendary *qasas* material collected by early Muslim historians, which itself was often mingled with Christian and Jewish lore. The earliest surviving document on the life of the Prophet, a papyrus fragment of a *sira* written by Wahb bin Munabbih (d. 732), includes many miraculous episodes that seem to be absent in the more matter-of-fact *maghazi* literature: the story of the spider web and the Prophet making a ewe's dried udder fill miraculously with milk. Interestingly, these stories in particular were not transmitted by sources normally considered reliable by early Muslim historians. *Sira* writers probably included them nonetheless because they provided ammunition against Christians disparaging Muhammad. They have since become some of the most recognized episodes in the Prophet's life among Muslims worldwide.

Many elements of the *Sira* seem designed to establish Muhammad (and thus Islam) as part of the line of Near Eastern prophets and as the pinnacle of holiness. In one report, Muhammad tells his Companions that 'Abraham was the friend of God, Moses was the Interlocutor of God (God had spoken to him on Sinai), Jesus was the Spirit of God, and I am the Beloved of God.' During his night journey to heaven, Muhammad meets all the earlier Abrahamic prophets. They follow him as he then leads them all in prayer. In an extremely bizarre story that Ibn Hisham cut out of Ibn Ishaq's *Sira*, the Persian Salman tells Muhammad that he had left his home in Iran seeking the true religion. Eventually, he came across a holy man in Syria who lived in a thicket. When Salman asked him about the religion of Abraham, he sent him to Arabia to await the prophet whose coming was foretold. Muhammad tells Salman that he was wise to heed the holy man – he was Jesus, alive and well!

In the *Sira*, Muhammad's interactions with leaders of other Abrahamic faiths could not be allowed to undermine his claims of ultimate prophecy. Historically speaking, however, Muslim scholars knew that neither the Byzantine nor Ethiopian Christian empires had embraced Islam. The *Sira* resolves this tension by portraying both the Negus and the Byzantine ruler Heraclius as secretly converting to Islam. Interestingly, we find this same literary phenomenon in Christian stories of the Muslim ruler al-Malik al-Kamil converting secretly before St Francis of Assisi (d. 1226) in Egypt.

One of the greatest challenges that Muslims encountered in their confrontation with Christians was the question of Muhammad's sinlessness. If Muhammad was truly God's last prophet whose religion had come to abrogate Christianity, should he not be the equal of Jesus and his mother Mary, in other words, sinless? Here the story of the washing of Muhammad's heart is most pertinent. The angels removing the black spot from his heart and resealing his chest represents the removal of sin, leaving Muhammad as pure as the immaculately conceived Mary and Jesus.

A closely related issue was whether Muhammad had ever participated in the polytheist religion of his people before his prophethood. If Muhammad was as pure as Jesus was in the eyes of the Christians, his infallibility and innocence could not have begun at age forty when he was blessed with prophecy. They had to be part of his very constitution. By the 9th century, it had thus become part of Islamic orthodoxy that the Prophet had never engaged in the rituals of pre-Islamic paganism. Even a senior Sunni scholar of Baghdad, Ibn Abi Shayba (d. 853), almost lost his credibility for suggesting that Muhammad had even watched pagan celebrations. The report in the *Sira* about Muhammad miraculously falling asleep instead of attending a rowdy wedding celebration seems designed to protect him from accusations of any pre-prophetic free-living.

Similarly, later Muslim scholars would insist that Muhammad had never eaten any meat sacrificed before an idol. Ibn Ishaq's *Sira*, however, included a report that as a youth Muhammad had once offered the meat of an animal slaughtered at a pagan alter to a *hanif* in Mecca. The *hanif* piously counselled Muhammad that eating meat sacrificed to idols is sacrilegious, and the young Muhammad decided never to do so again. Not surprisingly, Ibn Hisham removed this story from his edition of the *Sira*. Later Muslims, such as the great scholar of Damascus al-Dhahabi (d. 1348), would insist that the Prophet had never eaten meat slaughtered in a pagan manner. Any report recorded by earlier Muslims had simply been misunderstood. Muhammad may have slaughtered an animal in the proximity *of* an idol, but never *to* an idol.

Did Muhammad really exist?: revisionist history

Modern historians have generally concluded that, by reading the *Sira* in light of the various influences and agendas pursued within the text, we can sift out forged reports. Looking at the material that remains, we can retrieve an authentic kernel that represents the historical reality of Muhammad's career. According to this mainstream scholarly opinion, scepticism about the details of the *Sira* should not lead us to doubt its overall narrative.

Some Western historians, however, have called for more extreme scepticism towards Muslim sources. Known as revisionist historians, these scholars point out that we have no detailed history for Islam or biography of Muhammad for some 150 years after his death. Moreover, what we do have is all written by Muslims. These Muslims thus had over a century to manufacture whatever history they wanted about Muhammad and his faith. How then can we trust any Muslim version of his life or the origins of Islam? How do we know that Muhammad even existed?

In a controversial 1977 book entitled *Hagarism*, the historians Patricia Crone and Michael Cook argued that we can circumvent these challenges by relying on non-Muslim sources to reconstruct the origins of Islam. Not only were such sources not biased towards glorifying Muhammad, they were also much older than our earliest Muslim histories. Using Christian sources such as the writings of an Armenian bishop named Sebeos from the 660s CE, Cook and Crone contended that Islam was really a form of late messianic Judaism. Awaked to their Abrahamic roots, Muhammad and the Arabs had joined with the Jews of the Hejaz in an apocalyptic movement to retake the Abrahamic homeland of Palestine. Crone and Cook conclude from Christian sources that Muhammad was, in fact, still alive during the Muslim conquest of Syria.

The scholar John Wansbrough also argued that we can never locate the factual kernel of the historical Muhammad. All we can discover is the sacred history constructed by the Muslim community as it gelled in the late 700s and early 800s. In his books *Quranic Studies* (1977) and *The Sectarian Milieu* (1978), Wansbrough argues that it was at this time that the Muslims constructed the Quran and the *Sira* to create a religious vision anchored earlier in 7th-century Arabia. The life of Muhammad and the Quran were merely cobbled together from elements drawn from the Near Eastern religious heritage.

Based on archeological evidence, the Israeli historian Yahuda Nevo argued that Islam was originally a form of vague monotheism which only solidified into its 'Muhammadan' form after 692 CE. He points to a papyrus tax receipt from Egypt dated 22 Hijri/642 CE which begins with the formula 'In the name of God' but makes no mention of Muhammad. Nevo states that we do not see the phrase mentioning Muhammad until a coin minted in Damascus in 691 CE (72 Hijri) with the phrase 'Muhammad is the Messenger of God' (in fact, there is an earlier coin mentioning his name issued in 670 CE). After 692, however, Muhammad's name appears regularly in Umayyad coins and monumental inscriptions. The person of Muhammad before that time, Nevo concludes, must not have been a significant part of Islam.

Most modern scholars, however, object to the revisionist recasting of Muhammad and the origins of Islam. First of all, how were Muslims able to orchestrate a conspiracy as massive as rewriting the entire first century of their history? We must remember that during this time the Muslim community was wracked by civil wars and sectarian strife. Warring Umayyad, Kharijite, Shiite, and Abbasid Muslims could not agree on anything, let alone join forces to rewrite their collective history.

As for the absence of archeological evidence naming Muhammad before 691, it is not conclusive. Just because no earlier coins or evidence have survived does not mean they did not exist. Perhaps the Arabs continued their tradition of oral commemoration and did not record such things in written form.

Finally, the Quran itself is the most conclusive evidence that the Muslim narrative of Muhammad's mission is reliable in its overall structure. Unlike the *Sira*, the Quran bears no traces of civil war or sectarian propaganda. It never mentions Ali, Abu Bakr, or the Umayyads. Furthermore, there are no conflicting versions of the Quran. If the Quran was not affected by these forces, it must have taken permanent form *before* them. This means that the Quran consists of material dating back to the time of the Prophet or soon after his death. One person the Quran does mention by name is Muhammad, urging his followers over and over again to 'obey God and His messenger'. Muhammad thus seems to have been very important to Islam indeed.

We must also be cautious of uncritically accepting Christian descriptions of Muhammad's teachings. Christian writers may not have been biased *towards* Muhammad, but they were certainly not objective observers. They were describing the faith of the armies that had just steamrolled over them, so it is not surprising that they saw Islam and Muhammad in an inexact light. To rely solely on these Christian sources in writing the history of Muhammad would be like writing a history of the Soviet Union during the Cold War using only American newspapers.

More importantly, viewed together, these early non-Muslim sources paint a picture of Islam that does not actually differ markedly from the major themes of the Muslim version. The Greek historian of the 1st century BCE Diodorus mentions a temple in the Hejaz honoured by the peoples of Arabia, and the 2nd-century CE Alexandrian geographer Ptolemy mentions the Arabian towns of 'Yathrippa' and 'Mecoraba'. We thus know that Mecca, Yathrib, and most likely the Kaba existed long before Islam. Moreover, the Jewish historian Josephus (d. c. 100 CE) tells us that it had long been held that the Arabs were the descendants of Abraham through Ismail.

Non-Muslim sources certainly leave no doubt that a prophetic figure named Muhammad existed, and they provide an unsurprising description of what he meant to his followers. An anti-Jewish Christian text written in 634, just two years after

Muhammad's death, notes how the armies of an Arabian prophet had conquered Palestine. A Syriac Christian chronicle written in 640 mentions Muhammad by name. Writing in the year 687, the Mesopotamian Christian monk John of Phenak wrote that the Muslims considered Muhammad to be their 'guide' and 'instructor', who taught the Arabs to 'worship the One God in accordance with ancient law'. He remarks how strictly 'they kept to the tradition of Muhammad'. Another mid-8th-century Syriac Christian writer tells us that Muhammad went on caravan journeys to Syria as a youth. An anonymous chronicle written in the mid-700s in the Zuqnin monastery in northern Mesopotamia calls Muhammad the 'first king of Arabs', who considered him a prophet because he turned them from polytheism to worship of the one God. Muhammad gave them laws and they called him the 'Messenger of God'.

The Satanic Verses

The episode that has come to be known as the 'Satanic Verses' deserves special treatment. Made infamous in Salman Rushdie's 1988 novel of the same title, the Satanic Verses refer to an incident in the life of the Prophet in which he supposedly announced verses of the Quran which affirmed polytheistic beliefs and then retracted them. In the year 615, during the darkest time of Quraysh oppression of the Muslims, God revealed the Quranic verse 'Have you considered al-Lat, al-'Uzza and al-Manat, the third, the other...' (Quran 53:19–20), supposedly followed by the verse 'These are the high flying cranes, whose intercession is to be sought.' The Quraysh enemies of Muhammad were delighted by this because it acknowledged these three goddesses as noble beings to whom men could pray for intercession with the one great God – exactly the concession that the Meccans had been demanding of Muhammad.

According to this story, soon afterwards Gabriel informed Muhammad that this last verse had not been revealed by God. Rather, Satan had fooled the Prophet into thinking it was divine revelation. The verse was removed from the Quran and replaced by the verse that follows verse 53:20 in the Quran we know today: 'These [supposed goddesses] are nothing but empty names you have invented, you and your forefathers, for which God has bestowed no warrant from on high' (53:21–3). God then comforted Muhammad by revealing that 'We never sent a messenger or prophet before you without Satan intervening in his desires. But God abrogates what Satan interposes' (Quran 22:52).

The story of the Satanic Verses appears in the *Sira* of Ibn Ishaq as well as most early works of Quranic commentary (*tafsir*). Western historians have accepted it as true based on the HCM principle that reports that seem to contradict orthodoxy must be true (who would make them up?). As Watt notes, the Satanic Verses story is 'so strange that it must be true in its essentials'.

Indeed, the story seems to undermine central pillars of Muhammad's claim to prophecy: his status as an infallible channel of revelation and the complete reliability of the Quran. From a Muslim point of view, if Satan could interfere in the revelation of the holy book, how do we know that other verses were not also tampered with? From the point of view of a non-Muslim evaluating Muhammad's claims to prophethood, his 'error' in the revelation makes him seem like a mere mortal who first politicked to earn Meccan support and then tried to cover up a mistake.

We must be careful, however, in relying too heavily on the principles of the Historical Critical Method. Just because we think that a story makes an orthodox tradition look bad does not mean that the participants in that tradition viewed it in the same way. The great historian of the Prophet's campaigns, al-Waqidi (d. 822), reports that when Muhammad sent Khalid bin al-Walid to destroy the idol of 'Uzza, it came alive in the form of a naked black woman with long, wild hair. This also seems to contradict the orthodox vision of Islam. The Quran repeatedly states that idols cannot speak or defend themselves (see, for example, Quran 21:58–67).

Yet in this report we find one coming to life and charging its attacker. Should we believe that this story is true just because it contradicts Islamic orthodoxy? We know the story is not historically reliable – someone made it up. But why would Muslims invent a report which contradicted the Quran?

We must consider the possibility that early Muslims saw the story of the Satanic Verses, as well as those of live idols, as totally consistent with their religion. Certainly, most Muslim scholars later rejected the story of the Satanic Verses as heresy. The Spanish Muslim scholar Qadi Iyad (d. 1149) argued that the story could not have been true because none of the critics of Muhammad from the Quraysh ever took advantage of the episode to undermine his claims of prophecy. But other Muslim scholars accepted the Satanic Verses as fact. Some, like Ibn Taymiyya (d. 1328), explained them by saying that the Prophet was still entirely trustworthy as a medium of revelation because God would have corrected him whenever the Devil confused him. In the late antique world in which God constantly intervened in the lives of His prophets, the Satanic Verses would not seem out of place.

The *Sira* versus modern biography

Today, people pick up biographies to discover something intimate and essential about a historical figure. From the *Confessions* of St Augustine (d. 430) to modern works on Winston Churchill, the Western genre of biography provides a glimpse of the flaws and tarnish of human life. In discovering the imperfections and insecurities of prominent people, we often find that these private facets influenced them powerfully in their lives and accomplishments.

The *Sira* is a very different kind of biography. Muhammad in the orthodox Muslim view is a perfect man immune to human flaws. He acts as a prophet, leader, father, and husband with total confidence and is perfect in every respect. We sense very little of his own thoughts or inner turmoil. Even when his infant son Ibrahim dies and the Prophet sheds tears, his Companions react with surprise. He has to explain to them that he also grieves at such a loss.

Perhaps the only report that gives us a glimpse of the Prophet's inner ruminations is his terror upon seeing Gabriel for the first time, his thoughts of suicide, and ultimate refuge with his loving wife. It is no accident that the mention of suicide, present in Ibn Ishaq's original *Sira*, was removed in Ibn Hisham's more orthodox edition. That Muhammad could have doubted his calling or thought of suicide was unacceptable to Muslim scholars.

Another story which does not appear in the orthodox *siras* but remains in more expansive historical collections is a report of Muhammad's first love. While Muhammad was beginning his career as a merchant and before he met Khadija, he proposed to his cousin Fakhita. She rejected him, however, and married another man. This image of the young Muhammad as a youth rejected by a woman is perhaps the most 'human' of all reports about him, and it is no surprise that the *Sira* excludes it. As we shall see in the next chapter, the Muhammad that was so central to Islamic civilization in the manifold shapes that his persona took was far more than human.

Chapter 3
Muhammad in Islamic civilization

In September of 2005, the Danish newspaper *Jyllands-Posten* published a page of editorial cartoons depicting Muhammad in a variety of caricatures, from a bearded fanatic with a bomb in his turban to a comical figure welcoming his confused followers to heaven. The Danish paper saw this as an ongoing discussion on the status of free speech in Islam. Muslims worldwide received these cartoons as a deep insult to their Prophet. Protests and vigils were held from Turkey to Malaysia, and grassroots boycotts of Danish goods in Muslim countries led to a 15.5% drop in total Danish exports between February and June 2006.

This was not the first furore incited over depictions of Muhammad. In 1989, the Ayatollah Khomeini issued a ruling calling for Salman Rushdie's death following his portrayal of the Prophet as a manipulator living in a den of human frailties and vice in his novel *The Satanic Verses*.

How could a few cartoons or a fictional representation precipitate such reactions? The uproar provoked in these cases no doubt drew on simmering tensions over the relationship between 'Islam' and 'the West' as well as political and economic discontent within Muslim countries. The worldwide outrage that Muslims evinced, however, clearly represented something greater. Images of young Turkish businessmen crying at vigils held against the cartoons cannot be explained away as merely venting pent-up dissatisfaction. Similarly, Khomeini's ruling can be dismissed as extremism. But, as we shall see, it was an expression of the priority accorded to the Prophet's image in classical Islamic law.

We have explored the life of Muhammad, but nothing we have learned so far explains *why* so many Muslims reacted to the cartoons or Rushdie's novel the way they did. To do that, we must explore the roles played by Muhammad in the lives of Muslims in the centuries since the *Sira* was written. Here neither the orthodox image of Muhammad portrayed in the *Sira* nor critical attempts to discover 'what really happened' in his life matter. What matters is how Muslims have felt about his person. As you will see, that person has been central to Muslims' identification with their religion and an object of fervent love amongst the believers.

Muhammad in Islamic law and theology

Like Judaism, and unlike Protestant Christianity, Islam is a religion which places great emphasis on a detailed and comprehensive idea of holy law. The ideal of the Shariah (Islamic law) and man's obligation to obey it have been central to the way in which Muslims have understood their duty towards God.

The Shariah itself is not a legal code in bound volumes. Rather, it is the *concept* of a holy law. It has historically manifested itself

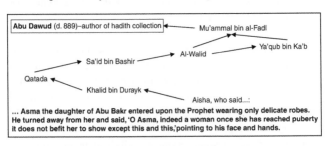

Abu Dawud (d. 889)–author of hadith collection ← Mu'ammal bin al-Fadl

→ Ya'qub bin Ka'b

Al-Walid

→ Sa'id bin Bashir

Qatada ←

Khalid bin Durayk ←

Aisha, who said...:

... Asma the daughter of Abu Bakr entered upon the Prophet wearing only delicate robes. He turned away from her and said, 'O Asma, indeed a woman once she has reached puberty it does not befit her to show except this and this,' pointing to his face and hands.

5. Hadith – why do Muslim women wear headscarves?

through the different schools of Islamic law (*madhhabs*): four Sunni and two Shiite. These were developed over the centuries by Muslim jurists whose main activity has been mining the sacred sources of Islam to develop a body of law that regulates all areas of life, from proper prayer to inheritance and the laws of war.

The Quran is the fount of Islamic doctrine, but it is not a legal manual. Only a small portion of its verses address legal matters, and even practices as fundamental as the five daily prayers are found nowhere in the holy book. Instead, it is the Sunnah of the Prophet that has provided the bulk of the Shariah. Muhammad's words, deeds, habits, and rulings are seen by the *ulama* (Muslim scholars) as explaining, implementing, and adding to the Quran. In both Sunni and Shiite Islam, the precedent of Muhammad has thus been indispensable.

The Sunnah of the Prophet was transmitted from him primarily through Hadiths, or reports about Muhammad's words and deeds. Recalled by the Prophet's Companions, Hadiths were transmitted from them by their students. This second generation of Muslims began setting down Hadiths, which had until then generally been transmitted orally, in written form in the early 700s. Along with the Quran, the legal rulings of the Companions and the legal opinions of the early *ulama*, Hadiths became a major component in the Muslim effort to answer the question that lies at the heart of the Shariah: 'Which actions are pleasing or displeasing to God?'

Hadiths functioned in much the same way as the historical *akhbar* (reports) we encountered in the last chapter. Comprehensive collections of Hadiths appeared in the late 700s, compiled by scholars like Malik bin Anas (d. 795) in Medina and Ahmad Ibn Hanbal (d. 855) in Baghdad.

The question of authenticity was at the heart of the collection and use of Hadiths. The Quran was collected soon after Muhammad's death and officially codified around 650 CE. There is thus no real debate over the historical integrity of the Quranic text amongst Muslims. Muhammad's Sunnah, however, was neither recorded in writing during his life nor compiled in permanent form soon afterwards. Instead, individual Companions and their students assembled their own private notes about the Prophet's acts and rulings. In the absence of any formal collection, thousands of Hadith were forged by various parties during the disruptive civil, political, and religious strife that wracked the early Muslim community.

As a result, Muslims were faced with the challenge of sorting authentic from forged Hadith. This presented a unique conundrum, however. If God and His Prophet know better than humans what is right or wrong and can know future events, how can mere humans know when attributions to Muhammad are reliable? For example, if a Hadith says 'the People in Islam with the greatest share of glory will be the Persians', is this a forgery by some Persian nationalist or really something that the Prophet knew would be true (the Persians have certainly been at the vanguard of Islamic thought)?

As a solution, the *ulama* developed a system of Hadith criticism based on evaluating the *transmission* of a Hadith instead of its contents. The chain of transmission of a Hadith was known as its 'support' (*isnad*). If a Hadith had an unbroken chain of transmitters back to the Prophet, if each of these transmitters was a pious Muslim respected for his knowledge and memory, and if the Hadith was corroborated by numerous people, it was considered a reliable saying of Muhammad and could be used as evidence in law.

Hadiths were also crucial for the elaboration of Islamic theology. Many theological tenets, such as the nature of heaven and hell, and narratives about the end of the world, come not from the Quran but from Hadith. For example, Muslims believe that

Jesus will return at the end of time to battle the Antichrist, a belief derived from Hadith such as:

> The Prophet said, 'The Last Hour will not come until you see ten signs', then he mentioned the Smoke, the Antichrist, the Beast, the sun rising in the West, the return of Jesus the son of Mary, may God's blessings be upon him, Gog and Magog and three great eclipses...

Muhammad as the centre of Islamic ritual

In the course of each of their five daily prayers, Muslims say,

> Peace be upon you O Prophet, and the mercy and blessings of God, and also upon all God's righteous servants.

They end their prayers by entreating,

> O God, send your mercy down upon Muhammad and the House of Muhammad, as you sent it down upon Abraham and the House of Abraham. O God bless Muhammad and the House of Muhammad as you blessed Abraham and the House of Abraham.

Taken as a whole, in fact, the Muslim prayer pays as much attention to the person of Muhammad as it does the individual believer saying the prayer.

Muhammad's most immediate role in the lives of Muslims worldwide has been as the centre of Islamic ritual. Muhammad is certainly not worshipped in Islam – only God is. But the Prophet's persona is the earthly pivot of faith and Muslim communal identity. The Quran and the Sunnah of the Prophet mandate this. The Quran tells the Muslims, 'Indeed God and His angels send mercy down upon the Prophet. O you who believe, send your blessings and bountiful peace upon him!' (Quran 33:56). Muhammad is quoted as saying in a famous Hadith, 'He who calls God's mercy down upon me once, God sends His mercy upon

6. Muslims in Malaka, Malaysia, awaiting the beginning of Friday prayer. Notice the cane lying in the pulpit; the Prophet would lean on his staff when giving the Friday sermon, so it became part of his Sunnah for Muslim preachers to do so

him ten times.' Another Hadith reads, 'The worthiest of people on the Day of Judgement are those who prayed the most for me.'

Throughout the Muslim world, it is customary to say 'May the peace and blessings of God be upon him' after mentioning the Prophet. As a result, during the Friday communal prayer any mention of the Prophet's name by the preacher during the sermon will elicit a collective murmur of prayers for Muhammad from the congregation. In such settings, the person of the Prophet becomes the common focus of Muslims' ritual attention. Remembering Muhammad and honouring his Sunnah act as the earthly focal point from which attention is directed upward to God.

Muslim scholars have gone to great lengths to encourage such ritual meditation on the Prophet. One Hadith forged by medieval scholars eager to promote this practice says, 'Whoever prays for me eighty times during the Friday communal prayer, God will forgive all his sins.' Pious Muslims often also print the above formula, praying for Muhammad after writing his name. Another Hadith made up to encourage prayer for the Prophet tells that if you write this formula after Muhammad's name, angels will shower prayers upon you as long as the book exists.

Outside their daily prayers, the persona of Muhammad has also played a salient role in Muslim religious life. A genre of literature known as *shama'il*, or books on the virtues of the Prophet, has been common reading amongst literate Muslims. They have also been some of the books most frequently read aloud by scholars to the less educated masses gathered in mosques throughout the Islamic world. *Shama'il* books parade the reader through the virtues of Muhammad's character, his extreme piety, and miracles. One such book, the *Signs of the Good (Dala'il al-khayrat)* by the Moroccan scholar al-Jazuli (d. 1465), is a collection of prayers to say for Muhammad and celebrating his remarkable character. In Egypt in the 18th century, it was the most commonly owned book after the Quran.

Muhammad as the paragon of virtue and embodiment of communal identity

In the *Sira*, we see that Muhammad is a man enjoying a special station with God, possessed of miraculous powers and foretold in Jewish and Christian scripture. He is still, however, a human being of this world. He errs occasionally in political or military decisions, and he is not omniscient.

From the 9th century onwards, however, Muslim writings about the Prophet outside the conservative *Sira* of Ibn Ishaq/Ibn Hisham elevated Muhammad's status into loftier strata. As Islam became the dominant religion in the Near East, Muslims absorbed the vast heritage of the Near Eastern world into a universal image of

Muhammad. He became the embodiment of perfection and totality. In a sense, as Muhammad's religion became the faith of the Near East, the heritage of the Near East became Muhammad. It would be this larger-than-life vision of the Prophet, not the Muhammad of the *Sira*, which would bind together Muslim piety and communal identity.

This medieval Islamic image of Muhammad was hyperbolic and even baroque, with his powers and character taking on extravagant form. The Prophet becomes perfect in every realm, sinless and without blemish. As a famous Spanish Muslim scholar named Qadi Iyad wrote in the 12th century, 'Know that if you look at the characteristics of perfection, those not acquired or earned but rather found in a creature's nature, you would find that the Prophet possessed them all ...' A 9th-century Muslim mystic claimed that Muhammad cast no shadow. Another report tells that when the Prophet relieved himself, the earth would swallow up his waste. It became accepted amongst Muslim scholars that Muhammad had been born circumcised. During the three days between the Prophet's death and his burial, Muslim scholars contended, his body was uncorrupted and preserved from bloating. One Muslim scholar reported that Muhammad had the sexual prowess of thirty men. Another claimed a more biblical forty. Other reports quote Aisha that Muhammad could see in the dark.

In the 9th century, Muslim scholars established the doctrine of '*isma*, or the Prophet's formal infallibility. Quranic verses and Hadith alluding to any mistakes on his behalf were interpreted away through elaborate scholarly gymnastics. Qadi Iyad, for example, explains that the Quranic verse stating that 'It is not for a prophet to take prisoners until he has established himself in the land' was not revealed to correct a mistake on Muhammad's part. Rather, it was only directed at prophets *other* than Muhammad (although, of course, Muhammad was the last prophet).

Beyond simply matching the wonders of Jesus or Moses, Muhammad became a hyperbolic miracle worker universally foretold. Qadi Iyad asserts that 'No prophet has been given a miracle except that our Prophet has one like it or even greater.' A report appeared that in the year of Muhammad's birth, God had granted the women of the world only sons in honour of the Prophet. During the Battle of Badr, Muhammad miraculously reattaches a Muslim warrior's severed hand. A 9th-century text tells of a pre-Islamic Meccan who visited a monastery in Syria and saw a statue of Muhammad there. Ancient Yemeni rock inscriptions in Mecca, hidden by the Quraysh, foretold his coming. In the 11th century, we find a story that even a pre-Islamic Arab soothsayer predicted the coming of Muhammad and his followers.

Not only had Jewish and Christian scriptures provided abstract predictions of Muhammad's coming, Muslim scholars argued, they had been explicit. A 9th-century text quotes an early Jewish convert to Islam explaining that the Torah reads, 'Muhammad the son of Abdallah, born in Mecca, emigrating to Yathrib, his domain will extend to Syria..., he does not requite wrong with wrong but rather grants respite after respite...' By the 12th century, one Muslim scholar claimed that this is actually the first line of the Torah. We should note that, although by 'Torah' Muslim scholars meant the totality of Jewish religious writings, there is no evidence that any Jewish scriptures actually contained these statements.

The famous biblical story of Daniel (Daniel 2) interpreting the dream of King Nebuchadnezzar becomes a prediction of Muhammad's advent. The Muslim version has the king dream of a monumental statue, its head of gold, middle of silver, lower part of brass, legs in iron, and feet from baked clay. Then God sends a stone from heaven and it demolishes it. The stone rolls on and grows as big as the horizon. This matches the biblical account, and, as in the Bible, Daniel tells the king that the statue represents a succession of great empires. In the Islamic version, however, he explains that the stone is the 'religion of God that He will cast against the nations at the end of time to make it supreme, and God will send an illiterate prophet from amongst the Arabs'.

Few of these stories appear in the biographies of Muhammad that became authoritative amongst Muslims during the 9th century, such as the *Sira* of Ibn Ishaq and Ibn Hisham. These stories are part of a later, medieval image of the Prophet in which there was no limit on glorifying the Prophet no matter how fantastic the tale. Muhammad's persona became the epitome of wonder and excellence, and even orthodox Muslim scholars felt that no accolades were excessive. As the famous 13th-century Egyptian poet al-Busiri wrote in praise of Muhammad:

> And attribute to his essence whatever honour you wish.
> And attribute to his station whatever greatness you wish.
> For verily the excellence of the Messenger of God has no limits
> That any speaker could convey with speech.

Insulting Muhammad

As Islamic orthodoxy gelled in the 8th and 9th centuries, the person of the Prophet became an embodiment of Muslim identity and community. This became clearest in the punishment that Islamic law decreed for those who insulted or belittled the memory of Muhammad.

The body of Islamic law is remarkably diverse, allowing for wide disagreement on legal rulings amongst the various schools. On the issue of Muslims insulting the memory of the Prophet, however, there was total agreement: the punishment was death. This was not the case for non-Muslims. The main position of Muslim jurists was that their punishment fell to the discretion of the ruler, just as the Prophet's ordering the assassination of some enemy poets who had lampooned was based on his calculations of what served the best interests.

Insulting the Prophet, however, is a crime for which the punishment has rarely been carried out. As with most cases of corporal and capital punishment in Islamic law, such as cutting off the hand of a thief, Shariah courts have historically erred on the side of caution and leniency. This infuriated a famous 14th-century Muslim scholar named al-Subki, who wrote a massive book on the necessity of executing those who insult the Prophet, after the Muslim ruler of Damascus granted amnesty to a Christian guilty of the crime. For the ruler, it was more important to avoid angering his numerous Christian subjects than to follow the strictures of the Shariah regardless of circumstance.

Furthermore, the Shariah has allowed for a certain freedom of religious expression for non-Muslims living under Muslim rule. The Christians, Jews, Zoroastrians, and Hindus living under the Muslim governments of the medieval Islamic world were allowed to practise their religions in security as long as they paid a tax. Of course, anyone who did not believe Muhammad's claim to prophecy was necessarily accusing him of lying – an insult to be sure. Since this was part and parcel of their religious beliefs, however, non-Muslims were not held accountable for this condescending view on Muhammad.

The Ayatollah Khomeini's death sentence on Salman Rushdie may seem barbaric today, but for a Muslim scholar like Khomeini, trained in the classical Shariah tradition, it would have been an easy conclusion to reach. Had not all Muslim scholars agreed on the punishment for someone who slanders the Prophet?

In order to understand the reason for this ruling, we must remember that from its inception Islam was founded on the person of Muhammad. The Muslim testimony of faith reads 'There is no deity but God, and Muhammad is the Messenger of God.'

Muhammad defines belief; Muhammad is Islam. Those members of the Medinan community who disputed Muhammad's religious authority during his life were expelled. Outsiders who defamed his person were usually marked for death. As Islam matured from a religious message into the framework for a whole civilization, the Shariah preserved the centrality of Muhammad to Islamic identity. To impugn Muhammad in the centuries after his death was to attack the persona that bound together Islamic civilization. It was a crime against the Muslim order, similar to treason, and not a matter of freedom of expression. Like treason today, it was also punishable by death.

Portraying the Prophet: images of Muhammad

One of the most frequently asked questions about Muhammad is the permissibility of portraying him in art. Like the issue of insulting the Prophet's memory, this question shows the disparity between the dictates of Islamic law and the realities of Islamic civilization.

Muslim scholars have uniformly prohibited depicting any living creature in artistic form, whether in sculpture or painting. This ruling is based in large part on a Hadith in which the Prophet states that angels will not enter houses in which there are statues. This sanction stems from a reverence for God and His role as the Creator; drawing or sculpting the image of a living thing is seen as acting like God. As another Hadith explains, those people who crafted such images in life will be asked to breathe life into them on Judgement Day or face damnation. In the modern period, Muslim scholars have allowed photography and film recording because these merely capture reflections of images and are not 'creations'.

Representing the Prophet falls under this broad sanction against portraying living creatures, but it has also received further attention from Muslim legal scholars. Although there is no explicit Quranic or Hadith evidence banning portraying the Prophet *per se*,

Muslim scholars have almost unanimously prohibited it. In a 1984 legal opinion, the Islamic Legal Academy of Mecca explains that portraying the Prophet in art or theatre presents a slippery slope to belittling him. This ban has generally been extended to the senior Companions as well. In the 1977 feature film *The Message*, the most ambitious attempt to transfer the orthodox *Sira* to film, neither Muhammad nor the first four caliphs were shown directly (in Shiite Iran, there seems to be more laxity in portraying Ali and the Shiite Imams).

In practice, however, artists in the Islamic world have routinely depicted living creatures. This began as early as the first part of the 8th century, when we find elaborate pictorial representations of the Umayyad caliphs on wall paintings and coins. Since then, Islamic art and illuminated literature have regularly featured pictures of animals and humans.

Pictures of the Prophet are rarer. The earliest known paintings of the Prophet are illustrations from a mid-13th-century Persian poem. A number of beautiful representations of famous episodes from the Prophet's life (in which Muhammad is fully portrayed) appear in the early 14th-century book *The Compendium of Histories* by the Persian scholar Rashid al-Din (d. 1318). Depictions of Muhammad became more common from the 13th to 16th centuries in Turkey, Iran, Central Asia, and India. The Prophet is often portrayed with a veiled face to avoid specific depiction, but art exists with his face portrayed. Of course, this does not in any way inform us how Muhammad really looked. Islamic art from this era was heavily influenced by Chinese styles, and Arabs and Persians alike are painted with the rounded faces and stylized features of Chinese art.

Muhammad and the mystical quest

Islam has always possessed a strong mystical dimension that underscores the absolute contrast between the ultimate reality of

God and the transience of His creation. As the Quran states, 'All things perish except the face of God' (Quran 28:68). Sufism, the Islamic mystical tradition, has affirmed that creation is nothing more than an ephemeral reflection of God's magnificence. Man's greatest accomplishment is to penetrate the veil of this world and 'become annihilated' in God in this life – as Sufis often say, 'to die before you die'.

For Muslim mystics, true piety and God-consciousness means seeing God's beauty revealed in every object in this world. The pinnacle of human awareness is to know God more and more intimately through His signs and perfectly reflect His attributes. To achieve this profound understanding is to completely reconnect with the source of all existence and fulfil the deepest yearnings of the soul.

This mystical worldview was first organized into a systematic cosmology, or view of the universe, by the seminal Sufi Ibn 'Arabi (d. 1240), who devised the conception of creation as a reflection of God's attributes. He cited a Hadith in which the Prophet supposedly quoted God Himself: 'I was a hidden treasure, and I wanted to be known. So I created the world and it knew me.' Every component of the cosmos and the natural world mirrors God's endless beauty, order, and creative capacity. The capstone of creation is mankind, which alone is capable of reflecting God's most essential attribute: His unity. The human soul embodies all the multiplicity of the cosmos but can also bring them into balance and proper proportion. A person who has achieved this state is the consummate reflection of God's perfection. This is the 'perfect human' (*al-insan al-kamil*), the ultimate 'knower of God' for which God created the universe itself.

Similarly, each of the great prophets sent throughout history reflected one of God's attributes, such as His power, creativity, or mercy. They culminated in Muhammad, whom the Quran calls 'the

Seal of the Prophets'. He was the 'perfect human' *par excellence*, the flawless reflection of God who represented the goal sought by all mystical seekers of truth. His timeless essence, which Ibn 'Arabi called the 'Muhammadan Reality' (*al-haqiqa al-muhammadiyya*) was the eternal reality of the 'perfect human' in the world and the whole purpose of creation.

In Sufism, then, Muhammad ceases to be a mere mortal. Behind and above Muhammad the man is Muhammad the cosmic reality. Practitioners of Sufism phrased this belief in several Hadith attributed (falsely) to Muhammad, such as the Prophet's words to his Companion Jabir, 'The first thing that God created was the light of your Prophet, O Jabir.' Another admittedly unreliable Hadith quotes the Prophet as telling that he existed as light two thousand years before Adam was even created. The timelessness of the Muhammadan Reality is demonstrated as the Prophet explains that:

> God sent me down to the earth in the loins of Adam, and made me of the loins of Noah, placing me in the loins of Abraham, and God did not cease moving me through the noble and pure wombs until He brought me forth from my parents.

The Prophet's ascension to heaven has provided a compelling model for Sufi mystical experiences. Reflecting the prophetic example, several prominent Muslim mystics experienced ascensions to heaven in a dream state. The famous Iranian mystic Bayezid al-Bistami (d. 874) dreamt that he was elevated up through the seven heavens, encountering the temptations of bliss in paradise at each stage. Like the earthly challenge of continually purifying one's behaviour and spirit as one progresses along the Sufi path, however, al-Bistami realizes that he must forgo these luxuries to move closer to God. Eventually, al-Bistami arrives at the highest heaven and encounters the spirit of Muhammad and the mystical presence of God.

Encountering Muhammad in dreams

In a famous Hadith, Muhammad is reported to have said, 'Whoever sees me in a dream, it is as if they have seen me while awake.' Based on this report, Muslim scholars acknowledged the reality of dream encounters with the Prophet. Visions of him in the dreams of Muslim scholars and laymen alike remain common today.

As we saw with al-Bistami, for mystics encountering Muhammad in a dream is a means for gaining mystical understanding. It could also influence Muslim scholars in their writings and legal rulings. In the 18th century, a Muslim scholar ruled that smoking tobacco should be discouraged after the Prophet appeared to him in a dream and told him that he did not like how Aisha smelled when she smoked (of course, tobacco did not appear in the Near East until nine centuries after the Prophet's death). During the Crusades, a Muslim prisoner who escaped from his Frankish captors told how his chains had been loosened by the Prophet in a dream. Some Muslim scholars believe that one can even see the Prophet during waking hours, although, as the great Egyptian scholar Ibn al-Hajj (d. 1336) said, 'This is a narrow door.' Strict laws of obligation or prohibition, however, cannot be based on dreams according to Islamic legal theory.

Muhammad in popular Islamic religion

In the Muslim world, Sufism has deeply affected the way in which the Muslim masses understand their religion. From Morocco to India, it is the popular devotion of Sufi brotherhoods and not the arcane discussions of Islamic law that has involved the masses.

The major Sufi brotherhoods of the Muslim world, such as the Qadiriyya brotherhood in West Africa or the Naqshabandiyya in India, emerged in the 12th and 13th centuries. They formed around the teachings of profoundly religious figures, like the Baghdad scholar Abd al-Qadir al-Jilani (d. 1166, hence Qadiriyya),

> Notice how this poem weaves the events of Muhammad's life together with themes of his cosmic significance. This poem has been an important part of Sufi ritual recitation and remains so in places like Egypt until today. The head of the Sufi lodge would recite the verses then all the brethren would join in for the refrain.
>
> I have transgressed the way of him who illuminated the night [with worship],
>
> Until his feet ached from the pangs of swelling.
>
> And he bound, out of hunger, around his belly,
>
> A stone over his fine skin.
>
> Lofty mountains of gold [were brought to] tempt him...
>
> Away from himself. But he turned away however high they might be.
>
> His earthly needs only strengthened his pious austerity in the face of such temptations.
>
> For truly need never prevails over the infallible.
>
> How can worldly necessities incline such a noble personality towards this earthly life,
>
> When if not for him this world would not have been brought out of non-existence.
>
> **[Refrain]: O My Lord, send Your peace and blessings always and forever,**
> **Upon Your Beloved [Muhammad], the best of all creation.**

7. Verses from the *Poem of the Cloak* praising the Prophet

who established sets of prayers, liturgies, and acts of communal devotion above and beyond the five daily prayers. These regimes of spiritual and personal purification solidified into Sufi schools, which in areas from the Balkans to India became the most prominent local religious organizations.

One of the most common communal liturgies among Sufi orders is reading the *Burda*, or the *Poem of the Cloak*, written by the 13th-century Egyptian scholar al-Busiri. Afflicted by a paralysing illness, al-Busiri was cured when the Prophet appeared to him in a dream and threw his noble cloak over the scholar's body. Inspired by the episode in the *Sira* in which Muhammad rewarded the poet Ka'b with his cloak, al-Busiri wrote an Arabic poem praising the Prophet in gratitude for his cure. Ruminating on the great moments of the *Sira*, the poem asks God's forgiveness in the name of the noble Prophet.

The *Poem of the Cloak* draws on the whole heritage of stories recounting Muhammad's miracles and infallibility as well as the Sufi characterization of him as a cosmic reality. 'Muhammad is the master of both worlds [this world and the next]', it reads, 'and of both domains [of mankind and the *jinn*]'. 'Can his true reality be comprehended in this world?', the poem asks, or, 'Like those asleep, can people only ponder him in dreams?' The poem underscores the finality and perfection of Muhammad's prophethood. 'Every miracle that the noble prophets brought before', al-Busiri writes, 'all were but derived from [Muhammad's] light upon them. For those prophets are but the stars, while truly he is the sun of virtue.'

One of the most important roles that Muhammad has played in popular religion has been as a channel for *baraka*, or blessing. We saw in the *Sira* that the Prophet's hairs, saliva, and even his blood were considered vehicles for blessings. They brought believers closer to God through a connection to the body of His Prophet. Like other tales about Muhammad, this quest for *baraka* took on a baroque and extravagant tone in the centuries after Muhammad's death. One Hadith was made up in which a woman who drank the Prophet's urine became immune to illness until the day she died.

After the Prophet's death, Muslims accessed the *baraka* of his person by visiting his grave in Medina or the graves of his descendants. Well-known Hadiths encouraged Muslims to pay their respects to Muhammad's grave en route to the *Hajj* in Mecca, quoting the Prophet as saying, 'Whoever visits me after my death is like one who visited me during my life.' Hadiths explained that when a Muslim greets Muhammad in his grave, the Prophet will return the greeting.

Some Muslim scholars have worried that devotion to Muhammad and the emotions stirred up at his graveside might lead people to worship him rather than God. As Qadi Iyad explains, visiting the grave of the Prophet should thus be a sober act: 'I do not see it fitting to stand by the grave of the Prophet and pray, but rather one greets him and moves on.'

Many Muslim scholars have advocated calling on Muhammad in times of need as a means of accessing God's favours. After being miraculously rescued from the desert, one Moroccan scholar named al-Tilimsani (d. 1284) wrote an entire book on invoking Muhammad's aid. Al-Tilimsani lost his way and almost died of thirst while travelling to Mecca. He was saved by a mysterious figure clad in white after calling on Muhammad for intervention. Seeking intercession from the spirit of the Prophet, of course, has proven controversial, and many Muslim scholars reject it as granting a human powers possessed only by God.

The *baraka* of the Prophet has also survived in the blood of his descendants, all through Fatima. For Shiite Muslims, this devotion to the family of the Prophet has been especially pronounced. In the 11th century, the grave of the Prophet's descendant Ali Rida (d. 818) in northeastern Iran became a popular pilgrimage location. One legend among Shiites holds that visiting the tomb carries the same reward as performing the *Hajj* seventy times.

8. **Women visiting the tomb of al-Husayn's head in Cairo. The entire edifice is silver**

Today, the Iranian city of Mashhad is built around the shrine of Ali Rida, and every year millions of Shiites come to pray and ask for blessings in the elaborate mosques surrounding the tomb.

Since the 11th and 12th centuries, the graves of various descendants of the Prophet have been 'discovered' all over the Muslim world. They have been honoured by Sunnis and Shiites alike. The head of the Prophet's martyred grandson al-Husayn was moved to Cairo in 1153, and eventually the al-Husayn Mosque was built over the tomb housing the head. Today, the mosque's ornate silver grave chamber is Cairo's most popular destination for visitors and locals searching for a connection with the Prophet.

The Mawlid: celebrating Muhammad's birthday

The Prophet was born on the 12th of the Arabian month of Rabi' al-Awwal, and beginning in the late 11th and early 12th centuries Muslims in the Near East began celebrating his birthday as a religious occasion. Interestingly, the Mawlid (Birthday) of the Prophet probably originated from earlier Shiite celebrations of Ali's birthday. In 1123 CE, the Shiite Fatimid dynasty in Egypt began holding public celebrations of Muhammad's birthday in which sweets and charity were dispensed to the public, preachers publicly recounted the Prophet's virtues, and the ruler led visits to the shrines of prominent descendants of the Prophet in Cairo. The Fatimids also celebrated the birthdays of Ali, Fatima, and the ruler of the dynasty, cementing perceptions of a link between the dynasty and the Prophet.

By the late 1100s, celebrations of the Prophet's birthday had become common amongst Muslims in the Near East based on a theme of thanking God for the blessings of the Prophet. Storytellers and preachers would recount tales of the signs prognosticating Muhammad's coming and the wonders of his birth and early childhood. The fact that these stories focused on the roles of women in the Prophet's life, such as his mother and wet nurse Halima, suggests that Mawlid celebrations were an opportunity for Muslim women to participate in public religious celebration.

Today, the Mawlid of the Prophet is a common celebration across the Muslim world. In Egypt, a carnival-like atmosphere reigns as brightly coloured tents and festive lighting illuminate the night and families stroll between food vendors. Popular storytellers in Egypt, known as 'praisers' (*maddah*), recount poems describing the Prophet in colloquial Arabic instead of the high literary language.

Although these *maddah*s speak in the common tongue, their poems weave together the complex mystical and historical strands of significance that collected around the person of Muhammad in Islamic civilization. We find, for example, a modern Egyptian *maddah* singing of the primordial light of the Prophet:

Adam is the father of all mankind, but the Prophet existed before him ..., [Adam] obeyed Satan once, and became full of remorse. When he sought the Prophet's help, the Lord then forgave him.

These Mawlid poets, however, take the miracles and station of the Prophet into realms far beyond the high tradition of Islamic orthodoxy. One poet tells the well-known story of the Prophet splitting the moon, but goes on to recount how the two halves of the moon entered and passed through the Prophet's sleeves before circumambulating the Kaba seven times like a pilgrim. At a Mawlid in the Egyptian city of Tanta, one modern poet went further and told of the moon not wanting to leave Muhammad's presence and remaining in his sleeves. The Prophet commands:

'Get out, O moon',
The moon answered the Prophet saying:

Muhammad

9. Celebration at a Mawlid in Cairo. What looks like a birthday cake is actually a cake of henna, a traditional dye used to decorate women's hands and arms

'Let me be with you.'

The Prophet said: 'Get out!'

The moon exited from his sleeves and prostrated to him.

Remembering the Prophet in song: South Asian Qawwali

Many Sufi brotherhoods developed rituals that employed music, dance, and singing to concentrate on God and induce states of spiritual ecstasy. The famous 'Whirling Dervishes' of Turkey are in fact adepts of the Mevlevi Sufi order. Reflecting on the person of the Prophet featured prominently in these ceremonies.

The tradition of Qawwali music, or the songs performed during such Sufi rituals, achieved a high level of sophistication in India beginning in the 14th century. Drawing on the rich heritage of Arab, Persian, and Hindu music in the region, Indian Muslims developed a school of Qawwali that continues to thrive in India and Pakistan today.

Qawwali groups today consist of up to a dozen singers and musicians playing drums and harmoniums (an instrument similar to the accordion). Performances usually occur around the shrines of Muslim saints or descendants of the Prophet, although wealthy families also invite Qawwali ensembles to their homes for private celebrations such as the birth of a new child. Sung in a mixture of Persian, Arabic, and the South Asian *lingua franca* of Urdu, Qawwali ranges from odes to the Prophet to love songs. The music is designed to move the audience into a state of heightened spiritual awareness and draw them closer to the mystical reality of God.

Like the *Poem of the Cloak* and Mawlid poetry, Qawwali songs draw on Islamic civilization's boundless reservoir of

Muhammadan lore. Even amongst Sunni Muslims, Ali and the family of the Prophet feature prominently in Qawwali songs. Just as Muhammad's eternal reality existed before creation, so it was passed on through his family. The song 'Haqq Ali Haqq' (Truth Ali Truth) became a popular hit of the late Pakistani Qawwali singer Nusrat Fatih Ali Khan (d. 1997), whose dynamic performances garnered him international acclaim. As the drums and harmonium reach a crescendo, Nusrat sings:

O Ali, spirit of the Prophet, body of the Prophet, life of the Prophet!
Why would Ali not be 'the Lion of God', 'the hand of God'?
The king of all warriors, Ali is intended in every favour.

10. A billboard in Mashhad, Iran. It advocates repentance and abstaining from sins in order to hasten the return of the Hidden Imam, a descendant of the Prophet whom Shiites believe will return at the end of time to bring justice to the world

Just as there is no one like Muhammad,
No other Ali could ever have been born...
...These five are the reasons for existence: Fatima, Hasan, Husayn, the
Chosen One (Muhammad), and Ali!

Muhammad in the modern world

The traditional place of Muhammad, the Last Messenger of God,
remains alive and well in Muslim life and practice today. Yet the
image of Muhammad has also taken on new forms with the
advent of the modern world. For Muslims from West Africa to
Indonesia, modern science, technology, and economy were first
introduced through the imposition of European colonialism. This
domination by non-Muslims confronted Muslims with a daunting
question: if Islam is God's chosen religion, and the followers of
Muhammad His chosen people, why are they so powerless before
non-believers?

To address this challenge, Muslim efforts to resist colonialism and
achieve parity with European nations in science and social
organization have often expressed themselves in Islamic terms.
The governments of modern Muslim states and Muslim
intellectuals have frequently advocated the adoption of modern
European ideas. But such modernization has often been phrased in
the language of Islamic faith and institutions in order to appeal to
Muslim populations craving a sense of cultural authenticity and
autonomy from the West. As it had in pre-modern Islamic
civilization, the person of Muhammad would serve as a crucial
vehicle for articulating Muslim responses to modernity and
colonialism.

Influenced by European historians, many modern Muslim
intellectuals have sought to present an image of Muhammad as an
historical person instead of the centrepiece of a sacred narrative.
In a wildly popular 1936 (since republished many times)

biography of the Prophet, the Egyptian intellectual Muhammad Husayn Haykal (d. 1956) presented him as an ideal but very human leader. Claiming to follow modern scholarly methods, Haykal dismisses the miracles of the *Sira*. He explains the defeat of the Ethiopian army before Mecca, for example, by a smallpox epidemic and not miraculous intervention. The story of the Prophet's chest being split and his heart cleansed is historically unreliable in Haykal's eyes. Ignoring the miraculous, Haykal prefers to explore the formation of the Prophet's character through his many painful human experiences such as the loss of his parents and children.

Modern Muslim biographers such as Haykal portray this historical Muhammad as a consummate statesman and role model for leaders in modern times. This Muhammad is an able commander and social reformer, not the miracle worker we find in the *Sira*. Amid the overpowering influences of European capitalism, socialism, and communism, Haykal portrays Muhammad as a man whose vision of a community based on faith and social justice provided a modern alternative for Muslims. Similarly, the popular Egyptian writer Abbas Mahmoud al-'Aqqad (d. 1964) wrote a book entitled '*Abqariyyat Muhammad* (*The Genius of Muhammad*) in which he hoped to demonstrate the Prophet's genius as a leader in the mould of Carlyle's 'great man' view of history.

The vision of Muhammad as the cosmic 'perfect man' has also assumed modern shades. Fethullah Gülen is a contemporary Turkish thinker whose writings have resonated widely in his home country. He presents a vision of Islam which he sees as uniquely progressive and moderate. Gülen's book *The Messenger of God Muhammad* presents the Prophet as the embodiment of this moderate and holistic vision. 'The problems of our time', he writes, 'will be solved by following the way of Muhammad.' Only the Prophet's model offers us the ideal healthy and holistic combination of science and religion, worldliness and spirituality.

Here, the 'perfect man' of the Sufis becomes the perfect citizen of the postmodern world:

> '...the Prophet Muhammad perfectly combined a philosopher's intellect, a commander's valour, a scientist's genius, a sage's wisdom, a statesman's insight and administrative ability, a Sufi master's spiritual profundity and a scholar's knowledge in his own person.'

In the mid-20th century, Muhammad also became the hero of the oppressed. In the tumultuous years leading up to the 1979 Iranian Revolution, the voice of the Iranian thinker Ali Shariati (d. 1977) carried massive appeal among Iranians. Combining a rich background in Shiite Islam, training as a sociologist in France, and Marxist leanings, Shariati critiqued Iranian society and the Muslim world as a people oppressed by a corrupt elite co-opted by Western greed. In his seminal Persian treatise *Islamshenasi* (Islamology), Shariati wrote of Islam as a force for philosophical and social renewal in Iran. Here, we see Muhammad portrayed as a social reformer and a Marxist liberator of the oppressed masses. 'Muhammad, a young orphan, who used to take the sheep of the Meccans to graze in the outskirts', Shariati writes, 'suddenly, from his sequestered life in the cave of Mount Hira comes down and declares war against the capitalists, the slave dealers of Mecca, and the farm owners of Taif'.

Muslim intellectuals of the 20th century also saw in Muhammad a role model for gender relations. Turning the European caricature of the Prophet on its head, the Egyptian Islamic feminist Aisha 'Abd al-Rahman (d. 1999) contended that Muhammad was not lustful. Rather, he was a paragon of male self-restraint who remained celibate until the age of 25 and was then committed to a rewarding monogamous marriage until his wife died. Aisha 'Abd al-Rahman wrote several works on the wives of the Prophet, demonstrating that their relationships with him were complementary and of mutual respect.

References

Chapter 1

The first chapter of this book is a digest of the *Sira* of Ibn Ishaq with the additions of Ibn Hisham. I have also included some reports from other 9th-century Muslim historical sources, such as the Hadith collections of al-Bukhari and al-Tirmidhi, in order to give a more representative exposure to material on Muhammad.

Chapter 2

For citations on pre-Islamic Arabia, I relied mainly on Robert G. Hoyland's *Arabia and the Arabs* (2001). For information on late antiquity, I am indebted to Robert Kirschner's article 'The Vocation of Holiness in Late Antiquity', in *Vigilae Christianae*, 38 (1984) and Peter Brown's article 'The Rise and Function of the Holy Man in Late Antiquity', *Journal of Roman Studies*, 61 (1971), as well as his book *The Cult of the Saints* (1981).

For information about marriage ages in the pre-modern world, I relied on the series *A History of Private Life* (1987–8), M. K. Hopkins's article 'The Age of Roman Girls at Marriage', *Population Studies*, 18(3) (1965), as well as A. N. Wilson's book *The Victorians* (2003). Aisha's statement about the age at which a girl can menstruate comes from the *Jami'* of al-Tirmidhi (d. 892), and al-Tabari's statement from his famous *History*.

My citations of Montgomery Watt's study of the Prophet's life come from his *Muhammad: Prophet and Statesman* (1961), and I used this book as a representative piece of modern Western scholarship on the historical Muhammad. I also used information from Ignaz Goldziher's *Introduction to Theology and Law*, tr. Andras and Ruth Hamori (1981) and M. J. Kister's article '"A Bag of Meat": A Study of an Early "Hadith"', *Bulletin of the School of Oriental and African Studies*, 33(2) (1970).

My references to Voltaire come from his *La Philosophie de l'Histoire* (1765) and *The Age of Louis XIV*, tr. Martyn P. Pollack (1961). For other citations from famous historians, I relied on James Froude's 'Scientific Method Applied to History' from his *Short Essays on Important Topics* (1872), Edward Gibbon's *The Decline and Fall of the Roman Empire* (1954), and Jacob Burckhardt's *Judgment on History and Historians* (1999).

For information on Christian polemics against the Prophet in the early Islamic period, I relied on John W. Voorhis's article 'The Discussion of a Christian and a Saracen', *Muslim World*, 25 (1935), Frederic H. Chase's book *Saint John of Damascus: Writings* (1958), and Georges Tartar's *Dialogue Islamo-Chretien sous le calife al-Ma'mûn* (1985).

My discussion of revisionist historians and rebuttals of their theories draws mainly on Patricia Crone and Michael Cook's *Hagarism* (1977), Yehuda Nevo's article 'Towards a Prehistory of Islam', *Jerusalem Studies in Arabic and Islam*, 17 (1994), and Robert Hoyland's *Seeing Islam as Others Saw It* (1997).

Chapter 3

For material about the Prophet outside the authoritative *sira*s, I relied heavily on Qadi Iyad's *Kitab al-Shifa* and al-Suyuti's *Khasa'is al-kubra*. In this chapter, I also referred to Nelly Hanna's *In Praise of Books* (2003) for information about the circulation of books about the Prophet in early modern Egypt, on BBC stories for data on the economic effects of boycotts caused by the 'cartoon controversy', and Oleg Grabar's article 'The Story of Portraits of the Prophet Muhammad', *Studia Islamica*, 96 (2003).

Marion Katz's book *The Birth of the Prophet Muhammad* (2007) and N. J. G. Kaptein's *Muhammad's Birthday Festival* (1993) provided invaluable information about the Mawlid, and Kemal Abdel-Malek's

Muhammad in Modern Egyptian Popular Ballad (1995) served as
my main source for information about the *maddah* praise poets
in Egypt.

I relied on a recording of Nusrat Fatih Ali Khan singing in Pakistan
and later posted on YouTube (http://www.youtube.com/watch?
v=hMgffKG6NtA, last accessed 3/2010). The *qawwal* he is singing in
the recording, 'Haqq Ali Haqq', was originally written by the South
Asian Sufi poet Bedam Shah Warsi (d. 1936).

For examples of modern Muslim thinkers reflecting on the Prophet,
I turned to Fethullah Gülen's *The Messenger of God Muhammad*,
tr. Ali Ünal (2005), Ali Shariati's *The Visage of Muhammad*,
tr. Abdalaziz Sachedina (1979), and Barbara Stowasser's article
'The Mothers of the Believers in the *Hadith*', *The Muslim World*,
82(1–2) (1992).

Further reading

A very useful resource for all aspects of the Prophet's life and legacy is *The Cambridge Companion to Muhammad*, ed. Jonathan Brockopp (Cambridge University Press, 2010). For those interested in more in-depth biographies of Muhammad from the Muslim perspective, Martin Lings's *Muhammad: His Life Based on the Earliest Sources* (New York: Inner Traditions International, 1983, and since republished in various editions) is moving and readable. A. Guillaume has translated Ibn Ishaq's *Sira* in his *The Life of Muhammad* (Oxford: Oxford University Press, 1955, since republished). Guillaume includes Ibn Hisham's additions to the *Sira* as well.

Readers interested in learning more about Muhammad's historical context should see Peter Brown's *The World of Late Antiquity* (New York: W. W. Norton, 1971) and P. Brown, G. Bowersock, and O. Grabar (eds.), *Late Antiquity: A Guide to the Postclassical World* (Cambridge, MA: Belknap Press, 1999). Robert Hoyland's *Arabia and the Arabs* (London: Routledge, 2001) is the best book on pre-Islamic Arabia.

For more on the debates over 'the historical Muhammad', Irving M. Zeitlin, *The Historical Muhammad* (Cambridge: Polity Press, 2007) is an accessible survey of the different historical approaches and theories. Uri Rubin's *The Eye of the Beholder: The Life of Muhammad as Viewed by the Early Muslims* (Princeton, NJ: Darwin Press, 1995) is the best read for those interested in seeing how the *Sira* narrative developed over the centuries as Muslims struggled to forge an Islamic identity. Fred Donner's *Narratives of Islamic Origins* (Princeton, NJ: Darwin Press, 1998) is the most authoritative work on the historical debates around the origins of Islam and Muhammad. Two collections of scholarly articles are useful for readers interested in more advanced and detailed readings on early Islamic historiography: Harald Motzki (ed.), *The Biography of Muhammad: The Issues of the Sources* (Boston, MA: Brill, 2000) and Uri Rubin (ed.), *The Life of Muhammad* (Brookfield, VT: Ashgate, 1998). These two volumes also include helpful editors' introductions to the field and its debates. For an accessible and enlightening explanation of how oral and written history interacted in early Islam, see Gregor Schoeler, *The Oral and the Written in Early Islam*, tr. Uwe Vagelpohl, ed. James Montgomery (London: Routledge, 2006).

For more on Hadith and Muhammad's role in Islamic law, theology, and mysticism as well as modern debates over the historical reliability of the Sunnah, see Jonathan A. C. Brown, *Hadith: Muhammad's Legacy in the Medieval and Modern World* (London, Oneworld, 2017).

For those interested in the more ornate and hyperbolic image of the Prophet in medieval Islam, *Muhammad Messenger of God*, tr. Aisha Bewley (Malaysia: Islamic Book Trust, 2006) is a translation of the famous *Kitab al-Shifa* of Qadi Iyad. Al-Tirmidhi's well-known description of the Prophet, the *Shama'il*, is translated as *A Portrait of the Prophet as Seen by His Contemporaries*, tr. Muhtar Holland (Louisville, KY: Fons Vitae, 2010), with beautiful calligraphy. Also, Omid Safi's *Memories of Muhammad: Why Muhammad Matters* (Oxford: Oneworld, 2009) is a fascinating narrative of the life of the Prophet and what it has meant to Muslims throughout history, with excellent sections on art and depictions of Muhammad. Kecia Ali's *The Lives of Muhammad* (Harvard University Press, 2014) is also a very accessible tour of the ways in which Muhammad's persona has been adopted into various intellectual and literary traditions in

Islamic civilization. For a spectacular read on Muhammad in the Sufi tradition, look at Annemarie Schimmel's *And Muhammad Is His Messenger: Veneration of the Prophet in Islamic Piety* (Chapel Hill, NC: University of North Carolina Press, 1985). Minou Reeves has written *Muhammad in Europe* (New York: New York University Press, 2000) on the history of Muhammad in the European imagination.

For collections of images of Muhammad painted by Muslim artists, see David Talbot Rice, *The Illustrations to the World History of Rashid al-Din* (Edinburgh: Edinburgh University Press, 1976); *The Prophet's Ascension*, ed. Christiane Gruber and Frederick Colby (Indiana University Press, 2010), an edited collection of essays on how the Prophet's ascension story has been represented and understood; and *The Miraculous Journey of Mahomet* (London: Scholar Press, 1977), which includes the pictures from a 15th-century Turkish manuscript on the *Mi'raj* from the city of Herat. The website (http://zombietime.com/ mohammed_image_archive/ has done a stunning job of collecting every sort of image of the Prophet from across the centuries.

Index

Muhammad

ISLAM
A Very Short Introduction
Malise Ruthven

Islam features widely in the news, often in its most militant versions, but few people in the non-Muslim world really understand the nature of Islam.

Malise Ruthven's Very Short Introduction contains essential insights into issues such as why Islam has such major divisions between movements such as the Shi'ites, the Sunnis, and the Wahhabis, and the central import-ance of the Shar'ia (Islamic law) in Islamic life. It also offers fresh perspectives on contemporary questions: Why is the greatest 'Jihad' (holy war) now against the enemies of Islam, rather than the struggle against evil? Can women find fulfilment in Islamic societies? How must Islam adapt as it confronts the modern world?

> 'Malise Ruthven's book answers the urgent need for an introduction to Islam. ... He addresses major issues with clarity and directness, engages dispassionately with the disparate stereotypes and polemics on the subject, and guides the reader surely through urgent debates about fundamentalism.'

> **Michael Gilsenan, New York University**

www.oup.com/vsi

READING GUIDES

Very Short Introductions

Whether you are part of a reading group wanting to discuss non-fiction books or you are eager to further your thinking on a *Very Short Introduction*, these reading guides, written by our expert authors, will provoke discussions and help you to question again, why you think what you think.